LION HOUSE
RECIPES
Lite

LION HOUSE LITE RECIPES

Compiled by Melba Davis

Deseret Book Company
Salt Lake City, Utah

We wish to acknowledge the contributions of the following:
Photographs: Russell Winegar/Panorama
Food styling: Teresa Earley
Preparation of food for photographs:
Melba Davis, Ann Sudweeks, Brenda Hopkins, Gene Willes
Dishes: ZCMI
Hand lettering on cover: James Fedor
Inset painting on cover: Rebecca Hartvigsen

Pictured on cover: Cranberry Punch (page 8),
Chocolate Buttermilk Cake (page 119) with Fluffy Divinity Frosting (page 127),
Sesame Green Beans (page 118), Arctic Halibut (page 75),
Dinner Roll (page 15), Crunchy Vegetable Salad (page 102)

Library of Congress Cataloging-in-Publication Data

Lion House lite recipes / compiled by Melba Davis.
      p.   cm.
     ISBN 0-87579-904-3 (hardcover)
      1. Cookery. 2. Low-fat diet–Recipes. 3. Lion House (Restaurant)
   I. Davis, Melba. II. Lion House (Restaurant)
   TX714.L557   1996
   641.5'638–dc20   95-51135
                 CIP

Printed in the United States of America
10 9 8 7 6 5 4 3 2 1

CONTENTS

INTRODUCTION

The Lion House. Its very name evokes emotional connections for visitors to and residents of Salt Lake City. Some dwell on the richness of its historical legacy; others reminisce about wedding parties, family reunions, and other special occasions held there.

But for almost everyone, the Lion House means good food. From formal catered receptions to children's parties to lunch or dinner in the Lion House Pantry, every occasion at the Lion House calls for meticulously prepared, beautifully presented, delicious dishes.

Many of those memorable dishes were "brought home" to good cooks across the country with the publication in 1980 of the best-selling *Lion House Recipes*. Now, the wonderful cooks at the Lion House have assembled another great cookbook, aimed at the way we eat today.

Advances in scientific research and nutritional information have consistently confirmed the health benefits of eating lighter. Food producers have responded with leaner cuts of meat, reduced-calorie versions of prepared foods, and standardized labeling of package contents. A person doesn't have to be a registered dietitian to create health-conscious menus; a little awareness can make a big difference. Simply by making a few changes in the ingredients we choose and the way we prepare things, we can save hundreds of calories without abandoning the dishes we love.

Lion House Lite Recipes makes it easy. You'll find many of your old favorites here, lightened up for a healthier lifestyle. Fluffy dinner rolls and flavorful muffins. Chicken Alabam or Cordon Bleu. Flaky pie crust with less than half the fat of most traditional recipes.

And you'll fall in love with the new recipes gathered here: appetizers, breads, main dishes, salads, and desserts of all kinds, all selected with an eye for great taste in a lighter version. A simple nutritional analysis at the end of each recipe lets you know just what you're getting.

Here are a few things you'll want to know about these recipes:

1. There are many versions of "light," "reduced-calorie," "low-fat," and "nonfat" products available in today's market. Food and Drug Administration guidelines dictate that "light" products contain one-third fewer calories or half the fat of the regular version. A "low-fat" product contains 3 grams or less total fat in one serving. A "fat-free" or "nonfat" product contains no more than trace amounts of fat in a serving. You'll want to read the labels carefully when selecting your ingredients. For example, if a recipe specifies "light mayonnaise," it has been tested and the nutrition information calculated based on the light, not the nonfat, type of mayonnaise. If not specified otherwise, the regular product is the one used.

2. Nonstick vegetable cooking spray is often a good alternative to fats and oils in sautéeing foods and preparing bakeware. Many of the recipes in this book call for this product. Nonstick bakeware will enhance the benefits even further.

3. Cuts of meat vary dramatically in fat content. The nutritional information given in the recipes based on the cut specified. Where poultry concerned, for example, dark meat can have twice the fat content of light. Beef round is much leaner than cuts from the flank. A serving of extra-lean ground beef contains less than a third as much fat as regular. Again, read carefully to be sure you are using what the recipe calls for.

Most of all, enjoy yourself, knowing that the wonderful taste of *Lion House Lite Recipes* is healthful as well as a delicious choice!

APPETIZERS AND BEVERAGES

Baked Chicken Strips

*1 pound skinless boneless chicken breast
   tenders or halves*
½ cup low-sodium chicken broth
¼ cup low-sodium soy sauce
3 tablespoons vinegar
2 tablespoons granulated sugar
2 tablespoons brown sugar
1 teaspoon ginger
¼ teaspoon garlic powder
¼ teaspoon pepper

Cut chicken into approximately 16 inch–wide strips
and arrange the strips in one layer in a 13 x 9–inch
casserole dish. Blend the chicken broth, soy sauce,
vinegar, sugars, ginger, and garlic powder. Pour
mixture over chicken. Sprinkle with pepper. Cover
and let stand in refrigerator at least 2 hours, turning
strips over occasionally. When ready to bake, heat
oven to 325 degrees F. Uncover dish and bake the
strips in the marinade for 10 to 12 minutes, basting
once halfway through the cooking time. Serve hot.
Makes 16 appetizers.

NUTRITION (PER APPETIZER):   44 CALORIES

TOTAL FAT	LESS THAN 1 g	(8% OF CALORIES)
PROTEIN	7 g	(63% OF CALORIES)
CARBOHYDRATES	3 g	(29% OF CALORIES)
CHOLESTEROL	16 mg	
SODIUM	157 mg	

Stuffed Mushrooms

1 pound medium-sized fresh mushrooms
¼ cup grated Parmesan cheese
¼ cup dry bread crumbs
¼ cup finely chopped onions
½ teaspoon oregano
¼ teaspoon salt
⅛ teaspoon pepper
1 clove garlic, minced

Wipe mushrooms with damp cloth. Remove
mushroom stems and chop them very fine.
Combine chopped stems with cheese, bread crumbs,
onions, oregano, salt, pepper, and garlic. Fill
mushroom caps with mixture, pressing it firmly into
the caps and mounding it on top. Place mushrooms
on an ungreased baking pan. Bake at 350 degrees F.
for 18 to 20 minutes or until heated through. Serve
warm. Makes about 35 appetizers.

NUTRITION (PER APPETIZER):   10 CALORIES

TOTAL FAT	LESS THAN 1 g	(24% OF CALORIES)
PROTEIN	1 g	(25% OF CALORIES)
CARBOHYDRATES	1 g	(52% OF CALORIES)
CHOLESTEROL	0 mg	
SODIUM	33 mg	

Baked Veggie Wontons

18 wonton wrappers
1 tablespoon light margarine, melted
1 egg
1 teaspoon flour
¾ cup chopped, cooked broccoli
¼ cup chopped, roasted red bell peppers
   or chopped pimientos
1 cup shredded reduced-fat cheddar cheese
¼ teaspoon onion powder
¼ teaspoon thyme
⅛ teaspoon pepper

Preheat oven to 350 degrees F. Spray 18 miniature muffin cups with nonstick cooking spray. Brush one side of each wonton wrapper with melted margarine. Press wonton wrappers into the sprayed muffin tins with the buttered side up. Combine egg and flour in a medium bowl. Beat with a wire whisk until blended. Add broccoli, peppers or pimientos, cheese, onion powder, thyme, and pepper; mix well. Spoon mixture into the wonton cups. Bake for 15 to 20 minutes or until mixture is set and wonton wrappers are golden brown. Remove immediately from muffin tins. Serve warm. Makes 18 appetizers.

NUTRITION (PER APPETIZER):   44 CALORIES

TOTAL FAT	2 g	(45% OF CALORIES)
PROTEIN	3 g	(27% OF CALORIES)
CARBOHYDRATES	3 g	(29% OF CALORIES)
CHOLESTEROL	18 mg	
SODIUM	63 mg	

Vegetable-Rice Quiche

1 medium onion, sliced thin
1 medium carrot, peeled and grated
1 medium zucchini, grated
1 cup low-sodium chicken broth
¼ teaspoon marjoram
1½ cups cooked long-grain rice
1 cup shredded reduced-fat Swiss cheese, divided
3 egg whites, divided
1 whole egg
1 cup skim milk
¼ teaspoon salt
¼ teaspoon pepper

Combine the onion, carrot, zucchini, chicken broth, and marjoram in a saucepan. Cook, uncovered, for 15 minutes over medium heat. Turn heat to high and continue cooking, stirring constantly, for 5 to 7 minutes, until liquid has evaporated to a glaze. Remove from heat and cool to room temperature.

While vegetables are cooling, preheat oven to 350 degrees F. Mix the rice with 2 tablespoons of the cheese and 1 egg white. Spray a 9-inch pie pan with nonstick cooking spray; press the rice mixture into bottom and sides of the pan, forming a "crust" for the quiche. Bake for 5 minutes, and remove from oven.

Beat together 2 remaining egg whites and whole egg with milk, salt, and pepper. Mix into the vegetables along with the remaining cheese. Pour mixture onto the rice and bake, uncovered, about 20 minutes. The filling will be puffed and set. Remove from oven and let set 15 minutes before serving. Makes 10 appetizer-size servings.

NUTRITION (PER SERVING): 149 CALORIES

TOTAL FAT	1 g	(6% OF CALORIES)
PROTEIN	9 g	(24% OF CALORIES)
CARBOHYDRATES	26 g	(70% OF CALORIES)
CHOLESTEROL	26 mg	
SODIUM	229 mg	

Cheese Ball

1 package (8 ounces) light cream cheese
1 jar (5 ounces) blue cheese
1 cup grated reduced-fat sharp cheddar cheese
1 dash garlic powder
1 dash celery salt
1 dash onion powder
1 tablespoon chopped fresh parsley

Beat cheeses together until smooth. Add garlic powder, celery salt, and onion powder to taste. Form into a ball and roll in chopped parsley. Makes 25 servings.

NUTRITION (PER SERVING): 59 CALORIES

TOTAL FAT	5 g	(70% OF CALORIES)
PROTEIN	4 g	(25% OF CALORIES)
CARBOHYDRATES	1 g	(5% OF CALORIES)
CHOLESTEROL	14 mg	
SODIUM	146 mg	

Salmon Canapés

1 can (8 ounces) pink salmon
¼ cup light mayonnaise
3 tablespoons ketchup
¼ teaspoon salt
2 drops bottled hot pepper sauce
¼ cup finely chopped green bell peppers
20 pieces melba toast

Drain salmon. In a small bowl, combine salmon with mayonnaise, catsup, salt, hot pepper sauce, and green peppers. Blend well. Cover and refrigerate at least 30 minutes or until well chilled. Spread salmon mixture on melba toast pieces; serve cold. Makes 20 appetizers.

NUTRITION (PER APPETIZER): 25 CALORIES

TOTAL FAT	1 g	(45% OF CALORIES)
PROTEIN	2 g	(36% OF CALORIES)
CARBOHYDRATES	1 g	(19% OF CALORIES)
CHOLESTEROL	7 mg	
SODIUM	134 mg	

Crab-Stuffed Celery

10 celery ribs
½ pound fresh crabmeat, flaked
1 cup peeled, chopped tomatoes
2 tablespoons finely chopped celery
1 tablespoon finely chopped green bell peppers
¼ cup fat-free Catalina dressing
1 tablespoon lemon juice
⅛ teaspoon salt
⅛ teaspoon pepper

Trim a small amount off the back of the celery ribs, so celery will sit flat. Cut each rib into 4 pieces (about 2 inches long). Arrange celery on serving tray. Mix together the crabmeat, tomatoes, celery, peppers, dressing, lemon juice, salt, and pepper. Fill celery pieces with crabmeat mixture. Makes 40 appetizers.

NUTRITION (PER APPETIZER): 20 CALORIES

TOTAL FAT	LESS THAN 1 g	(7% OF CALORIES)
PROTEIN	1 g	(16% OF CALORIES)
CARBOHYDRATES	4 g	(77% OF CALORIES)
CHOLESTEROL	0 mg	
SODIUM	45 mg	

Seafood Shells

Pictured on page 107.

12 ounces jumbo pasta shells (16 shells)
1 tablespoon vegetable oil
1 cup finely chopped broccoli florets
1 clove garlic, minced
½ cup low-fat plain yogurt
¼ cup light mayonnaise or light salad dressing
½ teaspoon dill
⅛ teaspoon salt (optional)
¼ cup shredded carrots
¼ cup finely chopped seeded cucumbers
2 cans (6 ounces each) crabmeat,
    well drained and flaked
Salad Supreme seasoning

Cook pasta shells to desired doneness as directed on package. Drain and rinse. Place shells upside down on a paper towel to drain them more completely and allow them to cool slightly. In a small skillet, heat oil over medium heat. Add broccoli and garlic. Stir and cook until broccoli is tender-crisp. Remove from heat. Combine yogurt, mayonnaise or salad dressing, dill, and salt in a medium bowl. Blend well. Add carrots, cucumbers, crabmeat, and cooked broccoli mixture; blend well. Spoon 2 tablespoons mixture into each shell. Place in a 13 x 9-inch baking dish. Sprinkle with Salad Supreme. Cover and refrigerate. Serve cold. Makes 16 appetizers.

NUTRITION (PER APPETIZER):   113 CALORIES

TOTAL FAT	2 g	(18% OF CALORIES)
PROTEIN	7 g	(23% OF CALORIES)
CARBOHYDRATES	18 g	(59% OF CALORIES)
CHOLESTEROL	14 mg	
SODIUM	88 mg	

Southwestern-Style Guacamole

1 small avocado
2 medium tomatoes
½ small fresh jalapeño pepper
2 tablespoons low-fat plain yogurt
¼ cup minced fresh parsley
½ teaspoon coriander
¼ cup finely chopped red onions
4 teaspoons lime juice
1 clove garlic, minced
½ teaspoon salt

Peel and pit avocado, reserving pit. Mash avocado in a large bowl with a potato masher until just a few lumps remain. Peel and seed tomatoes and chop them fine. Seed and chop fine the jalapeño pepper. Add tomatoes, jalapeños, yogurt, parsley, coriander, onions, lime juice, garlic, and salt to avocado in bowl; blend well. Serve immediately with tortilla chips, or, if desired, push avocado pit into guacamole to keep dip from turning brown, cover bowl with plastic wrap, and refrigerate. Makes 10 servings, about ¼ cup each.

NUTRITION (PER SERVING):   51 CALORIES

TOTAL FAT	3 g	(50% OF CALORIES)
PROTEIN	1 g	(10% OF CALORIES)
CARBOHYDRATES	5 g	(40% OF CALORIES)
CHOLESTEROL	0 mg	
SODIUM	120 mg	

Roasted Garlic Dip

1 large fresh garlic bulb, whole
1 cup 1% low-fat cottage cheese
¼ teaspoon freshly ground black pepper

Wrap the entire head of garlic in aluminum foil. Roast on middle rack of oven at 375 degrees F. for 1 hour. Remove garlic from oven and, when cool enough to handle, separate it into cloves. Pinch each garlic clove so that the roasted flesh slides out. Place garlic cloves, cottage cheese, and pepper in the container of an electric blender or food processor. Puree for 10 to 15 seconds. Serve with a variety of fresh raw vegetables. Makes 12 servings, about 2 tablespoons each.

NUTRITION (PER SERVING): 14 CALORIES

TOTAL FAT	LESS THAN 1 g	(13% OF CALORIES)
PROTEIN	2 g	(69% OF CALORIES)
CARBOHYDRATES	1 g	(18% OF CALORIES)
CHOLESTEROL	1 mg	
SODIUM	77 mg	

Black Bean and Salsa Dip

1 can (16 ounces) black beans, drained
½ cup chopped green onions
1 cup thick and chunky salsa (mild, medium, or
   hot, according to individual taste)
4 slices bacon, cooked and crumbled

Combine all ingredients, mixing well. Cover and refrigerate 1 to 2 hours to blend flavors. Serve with tortilla chips. Makes 24 servings, about 2 tablespoons each.

NUTRITION (PER SERVING): 41 CALORIES

TOTAL FAT	1 g	(22% OF CALORIES)
PROTEIN	2 g	(20% OF CALORIES)
CARBOHYDRATES	6 g	(58% OF CALORIES)
CHOLESTEROL	1 mg	
SODIUM	26 mg	

Salsa

Pictured on page 107.

3 medium tomatoes (about 1 pound)
½ jalapeño pepper (fresh or canned)
½ small red onion, chopped
1 clove garlic, minced
1 tablespoon red wine vinegar
2 teaspoons lime juice
2 teaspoons olive oil
¼ teaspoon hot pepper sauce

Peel and core tomatoes and jalapeño; remove seeds. Chop tomatoes, jalapeño, and onion, and mix together with garlic in a medium bowl. Add vinegar, lime juice, olive oil, and hot pepper sauce, and stir well. Cover and chill in refrigerator for at least 2 hours to let flavors blend. (Salsa may be stored in refrigerator for up to 1 week in a tightly covered dish.) Serve with tortilla chips. Makes 10 servings, about ¼ cup each.

NUTRITION (PER SERVING): 18 CALORIES

TOTAL FAT	1 g	(50% OF CALORIES)
PROTEIN	0 g	(7% OF CALORIES)
CARBOHYDRATES	2 g	(43% OF CALORIES)
CHOLESTEROL	0 mg	
SODIUM	5 mg	

Hot Spinach Dip

*1 package (9 ounces) frozen spinach,
  thawed and drained*
*1 package (8 ounces) light cream cheese
  (Neufchatel, not tub variety), softened*
½ cup shredded carrots
½ cup light sour cream
⅛ teaspoon onion powder
½ teaspoon dill
1 jar (2 ounces) sliced pimientos, drained

Chop spinach and mix it well with cream cheese, carrots, sour cream, onion powder, dill, and pimientos in a 1-quart microwave-safe bowl. Cover with waxed paper or plastic wrap. Microwave on high power for 3 to 5 minutes, or until hot, stirring twice during cooking time. Serve hot with crackers and fresh vegetables. Makes 32 servings, about 1 tablespoon each.

NUTRITION (PER SERVING): 26 CALORIES

TOTAL FAT	2 g	(67% OF CALORIES)
PROTEIN	1 g	(16% OF CALORIES)
CARBOHYDRATES	1 g	(16% OF CALORIES)
CHOLESTEROL	6 mg	
SODIUM	35 mg	

Cottage Cheese and Herb Dip

1 cup 1% low-fat cottage cheese
4 radishes
½ teaspoon grated lemon peel
*2 tablespoons minced fresh basil,
  or 1 teaspoon dried basil*
1 clove garlic, minced

Blend cottage cheese in blender or food processor until smooth, about 20 seconds. Scoop into serving bowl. Chop radishes and blend well with cottage cheese, along with lemon rind, basil, and garlic. Cover and refrigerate 1 hour or more to blend flavors before serving. Makes 20 servings, about 1 tablespoon each.

NUTRITION (PER SERVING): 11 CALORIES

TOTAL FAT	LESS THAN 1 g	(39% OF CALORIES)
PROTEIN	1 g	(47% OF CALORIES)
CARBOHYDRATES	0 g	(14% OF CALORIES)
CHOLESTEROL	2 mg	
SODIUM	43 mg	

Dilly Vegetable Dip

1 cup low-fat plain yogurt
3 tablespoons light mayonnaise
½ teaspoon Dijon mustard
2 tablespoons minced green onions
½ teaspoon dill
¼ teaspoon onion salt
2 teaspoons lemon juice
⅛ teaspoon sugar

In a small serving bowl, combine yogurt, mayonnaise, and mustard. Stir in green onions, dill, onion salt, lemon juice, and sugar. Cover and refrigerate for at least 30 minutes before serving, to blend flavors. Serve with assorted raw vegetables. Makes 24 servings, about 1 tablespoon each.

NUTRITION (PER SERVING): 11 CALORIES

TOTAL FAT	1 g	(42% OF CALORIES)
PROTEIN	1 g	(19% OF CALORIES)
CARBOHYDRATES	1 g	(40% OF CALORIES)
CHOLESTEROL	1 mg	
SODIUM	20 mg	

Bean Dip

½ cup chopped onions
1 clove garlic, minced
1 can (16 ounces) refried kidney beans
1 can (4 ounces) chopped green chilies, drained
¼ cup shredded reduced-fat cheddar cheese, divided

Spray a medium skillet with nonstick cooking spray and preheat briefly on stove. Add onions and garlic; sauté until tender, about 1 minute. Stir in refried beans and cook over medium heat, stirring constantly, until mixture thickens (about 10 minutes). Add chilies and 2 tablespoons of the cheese and continue cooking, stirring frequently, until cheese melts. Spoon into serving bowl and sprinkle remaining 2 tablespoons cheese over the top of the mixture. Serve with tortilla chips. Makes 24 servings, 2 tablespoons each.

NUTRITION (PER SERVING): 16 CALORIES

TOTAL FAT	LESS THAN 1 g	(6% OF CALORIES)
PROTEIN	1 g	(22% OF CALORIES)
CARBOHYDRATES	3 g	(72% OF CALORIES)
CHOLESTEROL	0 mg	
SODIUM	63 mg	

Tangy Shrimp Appetizer

3 cans (4½ ounces each) broken shrimp
1 envelope onion soup mix
2 cans (46 ounces each) low-sodium vegetable cocktail juice
2 cans (14 ounces each) low-sodium chicken broth
¼ cup lemon juice
3 cups finely diced celery
¼ cup sugar

Rinse shrimp in cold water and drain. Combine with remaining ingredients. Refrigerate overnight to blend flavors. When ready to serve, heat in a large saucepan. Ladle into punch cups and serve hot. Makes 30 servings, ½ cup each.

NUTRITION (PER SERVING): 33 CALORIES

TOTAL FAT	LESS THAN 1 g	(15% OF CALORIES)
PROTEIN	3 g	(36% OF CALORIES)
CARBOHYDRATES	4 g	(49% OF CALORIES)
CHOLESTEROL	11 mg	
SODIUM	618 mg	

Apricot Refresher

1 cup orange juice, chilled
1 can (46 ounces) apricot nectar, chilled
1 can (6 ounces) frozen lemonade concentrate
3½ cups club soda, chilled
1 quart pineapple sherbet

Combine orange juice, apricot nectar, and lemonade concentrate in a large nonmetal punch bowl; mix well. Refrigerate if desired. Just before serving, gently stir in club soda and scoops of sherbet. Makes 32 servings, ½ cup each.

NUTRITION (PER SERVING): 38 CALORIES

TOTAL FAT	0 g	(2% OF CALORIES)
PROTEIN	0 g	(2% OF CALORIES)
CARBOHYDRATES	9 g	(96% OF CALORIES)
CHOLESTEROL	0 mg	
SODIUM	7 mg	

Sunshine Citrus Punch

1 can (6 ounces) frozen lemonade concentrate
1 can (6 ounces) frozen grapefruit juice concentrate
1 can (6 ounces) frozen pineapple juice concentrate
2 cups water
3½ cups club soda, chilled
3½ cups ginger ale, chilled

Combine lemonade, grapefruit, and pineapple juice concentrates with water in a large nonmetal pitcher or punch bowl. Chill in refrigerator. Just before serving, add club soda and ginger ale. Stir to blend. Garnish punch bowl with fresh fruit slices or ice ring, if desired. Makes 25 servings, ½ cup each.

NUTRITION (PER SERVING): 38 CALORIES

TOTAL FAT	0 g	(1% OF CALORIES)
PROTEIN	0 g	(2% OF CALORIES)
CARBOHYDRATES	9 g	(97% OF CALORIES)
CHOLESTEROL	0 mg	
SODIUM	9 mg	

Cranberry Punch

Pictured on cover.

1 quart cranberry juice cocktail
1 quart apple juice
1 quart sugar-free carbonated lemon-lime beverage

In a large nonmetal pitcher, stir together cranberry and apple juices. Cover and chill. Just before serving, add lemon-lime beverage and stir gently. Makes 24 servings, ½ cup each.

NUTRITION (PER SERVING): 45 CALORIES

TOTAL FAT	0 g	(1% OF CALORIES)
PROTEIN	0 g	(0% OF CALORIES)
CARBOHYDRATES	11 g	(99% OF CALORIES)
CHOLESTEROL	0 mg	
SODIUM	9 mg	

Clockwise from top left: Whole Wheat Bread (page 13), Orange Rolls (page 15), Onion and Herb Focaccia (page 18), Fruit and Wheat Muffins (page 22)

Imitation Pink Champagne

½ cup sugar
1 cup water
1 can (6 ounces) frozen orange juice concentrate
1 can (6 ounces) frozen grapefruit juice concentrate
⅓ cup grenadine syrup (check label to
    be sure brand contains no alcohol)
1 bottle (2 liters) ginger ale, chilled

Combine sugar and water in a small saucepan.
Bring to a boil, stirring until sugar is dissolved. Cool.
Pour into large (3-quart capacity) glass or plastic
container. (Do not use a metal container.) Add
orange and grapefruit juice concentrates and mix
well. Chill in refrigerator. Just before serving, stir in
grenadine syrup and ginger ale. Makes 16 servings,
½ cup each.

NUTRITION (PER SERVING): 93 CALORIES

TOTAL FAT	0 g	(1% OF CALORIES)
PROTEIN	0 g	(2% OF CALORIES)
CARBOHYDRATES	23 g	(97% OF CALORIES)
CHOLESTEROL	0 mg	
SODIUM	5 mg	

Hot Spiced Cider

⅔ cup firmly packed brown sugar
1 teaspoon whole cloves
3 cinnamon sticks, broken
1 teaspoon ground allspice
1 gallon apple cider

Combine all ingredients in a slow-cooking pot and
heat to simmering point. Simmer as long as desired
(at least 30 minutes to blend flavors). Makes 32
servings, ½ cup each.

NUTRITION (PER SERVING): 119 CALORIES

TOTAL FAT	0 g	(2% OF CALORIES)
PROTEIN	0 g	(1% OF CALORIES)
CARBOHYDRATES	29 g	(98% OF CALORIES)
CHOLESTEROL	0 mg	
SODIUM	2 mg	

Dilly Tomato Warm-up

1 can (46 ounces) tomato juice
¼ cup sugar
1 teaspoon salt
¼ teaspoon garlic powder
3 tablespoons Worcestershire sauce
3 dashes Tabasco sauce
¼ to ½ cup juice from dill pickles
⅓ cup lemon juice
Chopped fresh chives (optional)

Combine all ingredients except chives in a large
saucepan. Bring mixture to a boil. Let stand to
develop flavors. Taste to correct seasonings.
Beverage may be served hot or cold. Garnish with
chopped chives, if desired. Makes 12 servings, about
½ cup each.

NUTRITION (PER SERVING): 44 CALORIES

TOTAL FAT	0 g	(2% OF CALORIES)
PROTEIN	1 g	(9% OF CALORIES)
CARBOHYDRATES	10 g	(90% OF CALORIES)
CHOLESTEROL	0 mg	
SODIUM	700 mg	

BREADS

Whole Wheat Bread

Pictured on page 9.

1 package (1 scant tablespoon) active dry yeast
3 cups lukewarm water
¼ cup molasses
1 tablespoon light butter, softened
1 cup white flour
6½ cups whole wheat flour
1 cup oatmeal
6 tablespoons nonfat dry milk
2 teaspoons salt

Instructions for Mixing with Electric Mixer: Soften yeast in 3 cups lukewarm water in large mixing bowl. Stir in molasses and butter. Combine flours, oatmeal, dry milk, and salt; add (¼ at a time) to yeast mixture, beating until dough forms a ball and leaves sides of bowl (part of the flour may need to be mixed in by hand). Remove beaters, cover bowl, and let dough rise for 1 hour in warm area away from drafts. Spray two 9 x 5-inch loaf pans with nonstick cooking spray. Knead down dough; divide in half and shape into loaves. Place in bread pans and let rise until about double in size. Bake at 400 degrees F. for 30 minutes or until desired doneness. Remove from pans and cool on wire racks. Makes 2 loaves, about 12 slices each.

Instructions for Hand Mixing: Dissolve yeast in ¼ cup lukewarm water. In a large bowl, combine remaining 2¾ cups water, molasses, oatmeal, and dry milk; add half of the white flour and half of the whole wheat flour, one cup at a time, beating well after each addition. Add yeast mixture, the remaining white and wheat flour, and salt. Mix well, then knead until dough is smooth and elastic. Place in a covered bowl in a warm area until double in bulk. Knead for 10 minutes to force out air bubbles. Shape loaves and bake as directed in electric mixer instructions.

NUTRITION (PER SERVING): 167 CALORIES

TOTAL FAT	1 g	(6% OF CALORIES)
PROTEIN	6 g	(15% OF CALORIES)
CARBOHYDRATES	33 g	(79% OF CALORIES)
CHOLESTEROL	1 mg	
SODIUM	214 mg	

Miniature White Breads

1 package (1 scant tablespoon) active dry yeast
1 tablespoon sugar
⅓ cup warm water (110-115 degrees F.)
2¼ cups flour
1 teaspoon salt
½ cup skim milk
2 teaspoons butter or margarine, melted

In the large bowl of an electric mixer, dissolve yeast with sugar in warm water. Add 1½ cups of the flour, salt, milk, and melted butter or margarine. Beat together for 3 minutes. Add remaining ¾ cup flour; mix by hand or machine to make soft dough. Knead on floured surface for 6 to 8 minutes, until dough is smooth and elastic. Spray bowl with nonstick cooking spray. Place dough in bowl, turning to coat surface with spray. Cover and let rise in a warm place until double in bulk. Spray two miniature bread pans (5¼ x 3⅛ inches) with nonstick cooking spray; set aside. Punch down dough and divide in half. Shape into two loaves and place in prepared pans. Cover and let rise about 30 minutes. Bake at 375 degrees F. for 30 minutes or until loaves are golden brown. Remove from pans and cool on wire racks. Makes 2 miniature loaves, about 4 slices each.

NUTRITION (PER SLICE):   149 CALORIES

TOTAL FAT	1 g	(6% OF CALORIES)
PROTEIN	5 g	(13% OF CALORIES)
CARBOHYDRATES	30 g	(81% OF CALORIES)
CHOLESTEROL	5 mg	
SODIUM	285 mg	

French Bread

½ package (1½ teaspoons) active dry yeast
1 cup warm water (110-115 degrees F.), divided
3 cups flour
½ teaspoon salt
2 tablespoons cornmeal (yellow or white)

Dissolve yeast in ½ cup of the warm water in a small bowl. Let stand for 5 minutes. Combine the flour and salt in a large mixer bowl. Add the yeast mixture and the remaining ½ cup water. Beat until the mixture forms a soft dough. (If necessary, add a little more water or flour to achieve desired consistency.) On a lightly floured surface, knead the dough about 10 minutes, until smooth and elastic. Form dough into a ball. Spray bowl with nonstick cooking spray and place dough in it, turning to coat all surfaces. Cover and let rise in a warm place about 1 hour or until doubled. Punch dough down; cover and let rise again until doubled (about 45 minutes).

Spray a large baking sheet with nonstick cooking spray and sprinkle with cornmeal; set aside. Punch dough down and let it rest 5 minutes on floured surface. Shape the dough into a loaf about 12 inches long, and place it on the prepared baking sheet. Cover and let rise until doubled, about 30 minutes. With a sharp knife, slash dough diagonally at about 1-inch intervals.

Preheat oven to 400 degrees F. Place a large shallow pan of hot water on the oven floor. Brush loaf with water and place (on baking sheet) on center rack of oven. Bake for about 30 minutes, or until loaf is golden brown and sounds hollow when tapped. Makes 1 loaf, about 15 slices.

NUTRITION (PER SERVING): 96 CALORIES

TOTAL FAT	LESS THAN 1 g	(4% OF CALORIES)
PROTEIN	3 g	(13% OF CALORIES)
CARBOHYDRATES	20 g	(83% OF CALORIES)
CHOLESTEROL	0 mg	
SODIUM	66 mg	

Dinner Rolls

Pictured on cover.

1 package (1 scant tablespoon) active dry yeast
2 cups warm water (110-115 degrees F.)
⅓ cup sugar
2 teaspoons salt
¼ cup light margarine
⅔ cup instant nonfat dry milk
5 to 6 cups flour
2 egg whites
1 tablespoon olive oil

In the large bowl of an electric mixer, combine yeast and water. Let stand 5 minutes. Add sugar, salt, margarine, dry milk, 2 cups flour, and egg whites. Beat together until very smooth. Add 2 more cups flour, one at a time, beating until smooth after each addition. Add about 1 more cup flour, ½ cup at a time (in your mixer if it will take it, or by hand), until it is well mixed in. Turn dough onto a lightly floured board and knead until it is smooth and satiny, about 10 minutes. Gather dough into a ball. Scrape bowl clean and spray it with nonstick cooking spray. Return dough to bowl. Let dough rise in a warm (not hot) place away from drafts until about triple in bulk. (In a cool oven with a pan of hot water on a rack under it is a good place.)

Use the last of the flour as needed on the board for rolling and shaping the dough. (Don't use it all unless you need it.) Turn dough out onto floured board and let rest for 10 minutes so it will be easier to manage as you roll it. Roll or cut into desired shapes. Place on baking sheets sprayed with nonstick cooking spray. Brush surface of rolls with olive oil. Let rise in warm place until double in size (about 1½ hours). Bake at 400 degrees F. for 15 to 20 minutes, or until browned to your satisfaction. Makes about 3 dozen rolls.

NUTRITION (PER SERVING): 101 CALORIES

TOTAL FAT	1 g	(11% OF CALORIES)
PROTEIN	3 g	(11% OF CALORIES)
CARBOHYDRATES	20 g	(78% OF CALORIES)
CHOLESTEROL	0 mg	
SODIUM	151 mg	

Orange Rolls

Pictured on page 9.

1 batch of dough for Dinner Rolls
2 tablespoons olive oil
½ cup sugar
4 tablespoons orange juice, divided
1½ teaspoons grated orange rind, divided
1½ cups confectioner's sugar

Follow directions for Dinner Rolls. When dough is ready to shape into rolls, punch down and divide in half. Roll each half into a rectangle about 9 x 12 inches, ¼-inch thick. Spread each rectangle with 1 tablespoon olive oil. Combine sugar, 1 tablespoon orange juice, and 1 teaspoon orange rind, and spread over dough. Starting with the long side, roll rectangle up, jelly-roll style, and seal edges well. Cut with a sharp knife into 1-inch slices. Twist and stretch each slice, then place on baking sheet sprayed well with nonstick cooking spray. Let rise away from draft until double in bulk (about 1 hour). Bake at 350 degrees F. about 20 minutes or until nicely browned. Remove rolls from pans and cool on wire rack.

Glaze: Mix confectioner's sugar, 3 tablespoons orange juice, and ½ teaspoon grated orange rind. Drizzle over rolls. Makes 24 rolls.

NUTRITION (PER SERVING): 207 CALORIES

TOTAL FAT	3 g	(13% OF CALORIES)
PROTEIN	5 g	(10% OF CALORIES)
CARBOHYDRATES	40 g	(77% OF CALORIES)
CHOLESTEROL	1 mg	
SODIUM	224 mg	

White Potato Bread

1 medium potato
2 cups potato water
1 package (1 scant tablespoon) active dry yeast
¼ cup lukewarm water
2 tablespoons honey
2 teaspoons salt
2 tablespoons vegetable oil
6 cups flour

Peel and dice one medium potato and place in a medium saucepan; cover with about 3 cups water. Simmer until tender. Drain, saving 2 cups potato water. Mash potato. Dissolve yeast in ¼ cup warm water in a large mixing bowl. Add potato water, mashed potato, honey, salt, oil, and 2 cups of the flour. Beat together for 5 minutes. Continue adding flour till dough can be kneaded into a smooth ball. Knead for about 10 minutes on a floured surface. Spray the large bowl with nonstick cooking spray. Place dough in bowl, turning to cover entire surface of dough with cooking spray. Cover and let rise in a warm place until double in bulk. Punch down and knead again for about 5 minutes. Return dough to bowl and let rise again. Spray two 9 x 5-inch loaf pans with nonstick cooking spray; set aside. Punch down dough; divide in half and shape into loaves. Place in pans and let rise about 20 to 30 minutes. Bake at 375 degrees F. for 30 minutes or until loaves are golden brown. Remove from pans and cool on wire racks. Makes 2 loaves, about 12 slices each.

NUTRITION (PER SLICE):   133 CALORIES

TOTAL FAT	1 g	(10% OF CALORIES)
PROTEIN	3 g	(10% OF CALORIES)
CARBOHYDRATES	27 g	(80% OF CALORIES)
CHOLESTEROL	0 mg	
SODIUM	197 mg	

Whole Wheat Dinner Rolls

1 package (1 scant tablespoon) active dry yeast
¼ cup warm water (110-115 degrees F.)
¾ cup skim milk
1 egg
3 tablespoons light margarine, softened
1 tablespoon sugar
¼ teaspoon salt
1½ cups white flour
½ cup whole wheat flour

In a large bowl, dissolve yeast in warm water. Let stand for 5 minutes. Beat in milk, egg, margarine, sugar, and salt. Add white and whole wheat flours and mix well. Scrape dough into center of bowl, forming a ball. Cover and let rise in a warm place for about 1 hour or until doubled in size.

Spray 12 muffin cups with nonstick cooking spray. Stir down the dough and spoon it into the muffin cups, filling about half full. Cover loosely and let rise about 30 minutes. Bake at 400 degrees F. until light brown, 15 to 20 minutes. Makes 12 rolls.

Variations: Add 1½ teaspoons dried herbs (such as basil, sage, oregano, or thyme) to the flour before mixing. Just before baking, sprinkle rolls with sesame seeds or poppy seeds.

NUTRITION (PER SERVING):   118 CALORIES

TOTAL FAT	4 g	(28% OF CALORIES)
PROTEIN	4 g	(12% OF CALORIES)
CARBOHYDRATES	18 g	(60% OF CALORIES)
CHOLESTEROL	18 mg	
SODIUM	92 mg	

Soft Bread Sticks

Pictured on page 45.

1 package (1 scant tablespoon) active dry yeast
1 cup warm water (110-115 degrees F.)
3 tablespoons sugar
1 teaspoon salt
2 tablespoons vegetable oil
3 cups flour
Yellow or white cornmeal
1 egg white
1 tablespoon water

Dissolve yeast in warm water in a large mixing bowl. Stir in sugar, salt, and oil. Add 2 cups of the flour and beat until smooth. Add enough remaining flour to make a soft dough. Knead on a floured surface for 6 to 8 minutes, until smooth and elastic. Spray bowl with nonstick cooking spray; place dough in bowl, turning to coat all surfaces with spray. Cover and let rise in a warm place until double in size, about 1 hour. Punch dough down and divide into 12 pieces. Roll each piece into a rope about 10 inches long. Spray a baking sheet with nonstick cooking spray and sprinkle with cornmeal. Place bread sticks one inch apart on prepared sheet. Let rise, uncovered, until double in size, about 45 minutes. Beat egg white with 1 tablespoon water; brush over bread sticks. Preheat oven to 400 degrees F. Place a large shallow pan filled with boiling water on lowest rack of oven, and put baking sheet with bread sticks on the middle rack. Bake bread sticks for 10 minutes, brush again with egg white, and bake 5 minutes more or until golden brown. Makes 12 bread sticks.

NUTRITION (PER SERVING):   151 CALORIES

TOTAL FAT	3 g	(18% OF CALORIES)
PROTEIN	4 g	(11% OF CALORIES)
CARBOHYDRATES	27 g	(71% OF CALORIES)
CHOLESTEROL	18 mg	
SODIUM	185 mg	

Multigrain Molasses Bread

1⅔ cups skim milk, warm (110-115 degrees F.)
2 packages (2 scant tablespoons) active dry yeast
3⅓ cups white flour
1½ cups rye flour
1½ cups whole wheat flour
1 cup stone-ground cornmeal
¾ cup pumpkin (canned, or cooked and mashed)
⅓ cup molasses
2 tablespoons light margarine, melted
1½ teaspoons salt

Place warm milk in a large bowl. Add yeast and stir until dissolved; let stand 5 minutes. Set aside ⅔ cup of the white flour. Add to yeast mixture the remaining white flour, rye and whole wheat flours, cornmeal, pumpkin, molasses, melted margarine, and salt. Stir until mixture forms a soft ball. Knead on a well-floured surface about 15 minutes or until the dough is smooth and elastic, adding reserved white flour as needed to prevent dough from sticking to hands. Spray the bowl with nonstick cooking spray. Form dough into a ball and place in bowl, turning to coat all surfaces with spray. Cover and place in a warm place to rise until double in bulk, about 1 hour.

Spray two 9 x 5-inch loaf pans with nonstick cooking spray; set aside. Punch down dough and divide it in two. Form each piece into a loaf; place in prepared pans. Cover and let rise another 40 minutes, until doubled in size. Bake at 375 degrees F. for 35 minutes. Bread should sound hollow when tapped. Remove from pans and place on wire racks to cool. Makes 2 loaves, about 12 slices each.

NUTRITION (PER SLICE):   162 CALORIES

TOTAL FAT	1 g	(8% OF CALORIES)
PROTEIN	5 g	(12% OF CALORIES)
CARBOHYDRATES	33 g	(80% OF CALORIES)
CHOLESTEROL	0 mg	
SODIUM	156 mg	

Onion and Herb Focaccia

Pictured on page 9.

3½ cups flour
1 teaspoon sugar
1 teaspoon salt
1 package (1 scant tablespoon) quick-rise
  active dry yeast
1 cup water
2 tablespoons vegetable oil
1 egg
1 to 2 tablespoons olive oil
½ red onion, sliced thin
1 teaspoon rosemary or basil

Coat a large baking sheet with nonstick cooking spray; set aside. In the large bowl of an electric mixer, combine 1 cup of the flour, sugar, salt, and yeast. Mix well. Heat water and vegetable oil in a small saucepan until very warm (120–130 degrees F.). Add warm liquid to the flour mixture, along with the egg. Beat at low speed until moistened, then beat 2 minutes at medium speed. Stir in by hand an additional 1¾ cups of the flour. Continue stirring until dough pulls away from sides of bowl.

Turn dough out onto a well-floured surface and knead in the remaining ¾ cup flour. Knead until dough is smooth and elastic, about 5 minutes. Invert bowl over the top of the dough and allow it to sit for 5 minutes. Place dough on prepared baking sheet and roll or press into a 12-inch circle.

Spray a length of plastic wrap with nonstick cooking spray and cover dough loosely; gently place a cloth dish towel over the wrap. Let dough rise in a warm place until double in bulk, about 30 minutes. Remove cover from dough. With your finger or the handle of a wooden spoon, poke holes in dough 1 inch apart. Drizzle olive oil over top of dough. Separate onion slices into rings and arrange on loaf; sprinkle evenly with rosemary or basil. Bake at 400 degrees F. for 20 to 25 minutes or until golden brown. Remove immediately from baking sheet and cool on wire rack. Makes 16 servings.

Note: Focaccia is extremely versatile and can be flavored with many different herbs, onions, and cheeses, so experiment with your favorites. To freeze, wrap cooled loaf in plastic wrap or aluminum foil and store in freezer for up to 3 months.

NUTRITION (PER SERVING): 136 CALORIES

TOTAL FAT	4 g	(27% OF CALORIES)
PROTEIN	4 g	(12% OF CALORIES)
CARBOHYDRATES	21 g	(61% OF CALORIES)
CHOLESTEROL	13 mg	
SODIUM	139 mg	

Cottage Cheese and Parmesan Bread

¾ cup skim milk, warm (110-115 degrees F.)
1 tablespoon honey
½ package (1½ teaspoons) active dry yeast
3 cups flour
½ teaspoon salt
½ cup 1% low-fat cottage cheese
⅓ cup grated Parmesan cheese
1 tablespoon skim milk

Stir ¾ cup warm milk and honey together. Add yeast and let stand until bubbly, about 5 minutes; then stir until yeast is dissolved. Combine flour and salt in large bowl. Add the yeast mixture and the cottage cheese. Beat with a spoon until a soft dough is formed. Knead dough on a lightly floured surface until smooth and elastic, about 8 to 10 minutes. Spray bowl with nonstick cooking spray. Shape dough into a ball and place it in the bowl, turning to coat all surfaces with the spray. Cover and let rise in a warm place until doubled, about 1 hour.

Spray a 9 x 5-inch loaf pan lightly with the cooking spray. Punch down dough and knead in the Parmesan cheese. Shape dough into a loaf and place it in prepared pan. Cover and let rise for another 40 minutes, or until almost doubled in bulk. Brush loaf with 1 tablespoon milk and bake at 375 degrees F. for about 35 minutes. Bread should be golden brown and sound hollow when tapped. Remove from pan and cool on wire rack. Makes one loaf, about 12 slices.

NUTRITION (PER SLICE):   141 CALORIES

TOTAL FAT	1 g	(6% OF CALORIES)
PROTEIN	6 g	(17% OF CALORIES)
CARBOHYDRATES	27 g	(77% OF CALORIES)
CHOLESTEROL	2 mg	
SODIUM	178 mg	

Spinach Rolls

1 package (10 ounces) frozen spinach,
*   thawed and squeezed dry*
½ cup reduced-fat Monterey Jack cheese
4 tablespoons Parmesan cheese, divided
1 egg
2 tablespoons dried minced onions
1 pound frozen bread dough, thawed (not risen)
1 tablespoon light butter or margarine, melted

Chop spinach. In a medium bowl, mix spinach, Monterey Jack cheese, 2 tablespoons of the Parmesan cheese, egg, and onions. Set aside. Roll thawed bread dough into a rectangle, about 8 x 12 inches. Spread spinach mixture over dough and roll up, starting with long side. Pinch edges to seal. Spray a 13 x 9-inch baking dish with nonstick cooking spray. Cut dough in 1-inch slices and place in pan. Brush tops of rolls with butter or margarine and sprinkle with remaining 2 tablespoons Parmesan cheese. Bake at 350 degrees F. for 20 minutes. Makes 12 rolls.

NUTRITION (PER SERVING): 148 CALORIES

TOTAL FAT	5 g	(32% OF CALORIES)
PROTEIN	6 g	(16% OF CALORIES)
CARBOHYDRATES	19 g	(52% OF CALORIES)
CHOLESTEROL	28 mg	
SODIUM	494 mg	

Old-Fashioned Corn Bread

Pictured on page 27.

1 cup yellow cornmeal
¾ cup flour
2½ teaspoons baking powder
½ teaspoon sugar
¼ teaspoon salt
¼ cup light margarine, melted
1 cup skim milk
1 egg

Spray an 8-inch square pan with nonstick cooking spray; set aside. Combine the cornmeal, flour, baking powder, sugar, and salt in a medium bowl. In a small bowl whisk together the melted margarine, milk, and egg. Add to the dry ingredients and stir just until moistened. Pour batter into prepared pan and bake at 400 degrees F. for 18 to 20 minutes or until bread springs back when touched in middle. Serve hot. Makes 9 servings.

NUTRITION (PER SERVING): 131 CALORIES

TOTAL FAT	3 g	(21% OF CALORIES)
PROTEIN	4 g	(12% OF CALORIES)
CARBOHYDRATES	22 g	(67% OF CALORIES)
CHOLESTEROL	24 mg	
SODIUM	243 mg	

Cornmeal and Brown Sugar Muffins

½ cup firmly packed brown sugar
¼ cup white cornmeal
2 cups flour
1 teaspoon baking powder
1 teaspoon baking soda
¼ teaspoon salt
1 cup low-fat vanilla yogurt
3 tablespoons skim milk
1 tablespoon margarine, melted
1 teaspoon vanilla
1 egg
1 tablespoon brown sugar
2 teaspoons white cornmeal

Preheat oven to 400 degrees F. Spray 12 muffin cups with nonstick cooking spray; set aside. In a medium bowl, stir together ½ cup brown sugar, ¼ cup cornmeal, flour, baking powder, baking soda, and salt. Make a well in center of dry mixture. Combine yogurt, milk, melted margarine, vanilla, and egg. Pour into well in dry ingredients and stir just until moistened. Spoon batter evenly into the prepared muffin tins. Combine 1 tablespoon brown sugar with 2 teaspoons cornmeal; sprinkle over tops of muffins. Bake for 15 to 18 minutes, or until a wooden toothpick inserted in the center of a muffin comes out clean. Remove muffins immediately from pans and cool on wire racks. Makes 12 muffins.

NUTRITION (PER SERVING): 147 CALORIES

TOTAL FAT	2 g	(11% OF CALORIES)
PROTEIN	4 g	(10% OF CALORIES)
CARBOHYDRATES	29 g	(79% OF CALORIES)
CHOLESTEROL	19 mg	
SODIUM	179 mg	

Apple Cinnamon Muffins

2 cups flour
6 tablespoons firmly packed brown sugar
1 teaspoon baking powder
½ teaspoon baking soda
½ teaspoon cinnamon
¼ teaspoon salt
1½ cups peeled and shredded apples
½ cup nonfat buttermilk
1 tablespoon vegetable oil
1 teaspoon vanilla
1 egg

Preheat oven to 400 degrees F. Spray 12 muffin cups with nonstick cooking spray; set aside. In a large bowl, stir together flour, brown sugar, baking powder, baking soda, cinnamon, and salt. Make a well in the center of the dry mixture. In a separate bowl, mix together apples, buttermilk, oil, vanilla, and egg. Pour into well in dry ingredients and stir just until moistened. Spoon into prepared muffin cups and bake for 17 to 20 minutes, or until a wooden pick inserted in the center of a muffin comes out clean. Remove muffins immediately from pans and cool on wire racks. Makes 12 muffins.

NUTRITION (PER SERVING): 118 CALORIES

TOTAL FAT	2 g	(15% OF CALORIES)
PROTEIN	3 g	(10% OF CALORIES)
CARBOHYDRATES	22 g	(75% OF CALORIES)
CHOLESTEROL	18 mg	
SODIUM	125 mg	

Blueberry Muffins

2 cups flour
⅓ cup sugar
1 teaspoon baking powder
1 teaspoon baking soda
¼ teaspoon salt
¼ cup orange juice
1 cup low-fat vanilla yogurt
1 teaspoon vanilla
2 tablespoons vegetable oil
1 egg
⅔ cup blueberries, frozen or fresh
1 tablespoon sugar

Preheat oven to 400 degrees F. Spray 12 muffin cups with nonstick cooking spray; set aside. In a large bowl, combine flour, ⅓ cup sugar, baking powder, baking soda, and salt. Make a well in center of dry mixture. In a separate bowl, mix together orange juice, yogurt, vanilla, oil, and egg. Pour into well in dry ingredients and stir just until moistened. Fold in blueberries. Spoon batter into prepared muffin cups and sprinkle 1 tablespoon of sugar over tops of muffins. Bake for 17 to 20 minutes, or until golden. Remove muffins immediately from pans and cool on wire racks. Makes 12 muffins.

NUTRITION (PER SERVING): 155 CALORIES

TOTAL FAT	3 g	(19% OF CALORIES)
PROTEIN	4 g	(9% OF CALORIES)
CARBOHYDRATES	28 g	(72% OF CALORIES)
CHOLESTEROL	19 mg	
SODIUM	164 mg	

Fruit and Wheat Muffins

Pictured on page 9.

1 cup white flour
¼ cup whole wheat flour
⅓ cup sugar
1½ teaspoons baking powder
¼ teaspoon baking soda
⅛ teaspoon salt
1 cup peeled, finely chopped Granny Smith apples
¼ cup chopped pitted dates
¼ cup low-fat buttermilk
2 tablespoons vegetable oil
1 egg, lightly beaten

Preheat oven to 375 degrees F. Spray 12 muffin cups with nonstick cooking spray; set aside. In a large bowl, stir together the flours, sugar, baking powder, baking soda, and salt. Mix in apples and dates. Make a well in dry ingredients. In a separate bowl, combine buttermilk, oil, and egg. Pour into well in dry ingredients; stir just until moistened. Spoon batter into prepared muffin cups. Bake for about 20 minutes or until golden brown. Remove immediately from pans and cool on wire racks. Makes 12 muffins.

NUTRITION (PER SERVING):   115 CALORIES

TOTAL FAT	3 g	(24% OF CALORIES)
PROTEIN	2 G	(8% OF CALORIES)
CARBOHYDRATES	20 g	(69% OF CALORIES)
CHOLESTEROL	18 mg	
SODIUM	97 mg	

Cranberry Bread

2 cups flour
1 teaspoon salt
½ teaspoon baking powder
½ teaspoon baking soda
1 cup sugar
2 egg whites
2 tablespoons hot water
2 tablespoons olive oil
½ cup orange juice
½ cup chopped walnuts
1 cup coarsely chopped fresh cranberries
2 tablespoons grated orange rind

Spray an 8 x 4-inch loaf pan with nonstick cooking spray; set aside. Sift together flour, salt, baking powder, baking soda, and sugar. Make a well in the center of dry mixture. In a separate bowl, mix together egg whites, water, olive oil, and orange juice. Pour into well in dry ingredients and stir just until moistened. Fold in nuts, cranberries, and orange rind. Bake at 325 degrees F. for about 1 hour, or until toothpick inserted in center comes out clean. Let stand in pan for 10 minutes, then turn out onto wire rack to cool. Wrap loaf in plastic wrap or aluminum foil, and refrigerate 24 hours before slicing. Makes 1 loaf, about 12 slices.

NUTRITION (PER SLICE):   208 CALORIES

TOTAL FAT	6 g	(24% OF CALORIES)
PROTEIN	4 g	(7% OF CALORIES)
CARBOHYDRATES	36 g	(69% OF CALORIES)
CHOLESTEROL	0 mg	
SODIUM	255 mg	

Zucchini Bread

½ cup olive oil
2 cups sugar
6 egg whites
3 teaspoons vanilla
2 cups shredded raw zucchini
3 cups flour
3 teaspoons cinnamon
1 teaspoon baking soda
1 teaspoon salt
¼ teaspoon baking powder

Spray two 9 x 5-inch loaf pans with nonstick cooking spray and lightly flour them; set aside. In the large bowl of an electric mixer, combine oil, sugar, and egg whites. Beat well. Blend in vanilla and zucchini. Sift together flour, cinnamon, baking soda, salt, and baking powder. Add to zucchini mixture and blend well. Pour batter into prepared loaf pans. Bake at 350 degrees F. for about 1 hour, or until toothpick inserted in center comes out clean. Let stand in pans for 10 minutes, then turn out on wire racks to cool. Makes 2 loaves, about 16 slices each.

NUTRITION (PER SLICE):		123 CALORIES
TOTAL FAT	3 g	(22% OF CALORIES)
PROTEIN	2 g	(7% OF CALORIES)
CARBOHYDRATES	22 g	(71% OF CALORIES)
CHOLESTEROL	0 mg	
SODIUM	120 mg	

Spiced Quick Bread

1 cup white flour
½ cup whole wheat flour
½ teaspoon baking soda
½ teaspoon cinnamon
¼ teaspoon nutmeg
¼ teaspoon salt
1 egg
½ cup sugar
1 cup nonfat buttermilk
1 tablespoon vegetable oil
½ cup chopped pitted prunes or raisins

Spray a 9 x 5-inch loaf pan with nonstick cooking spray and lightly flour it; set aside. Stir together the flours, baking soda, cinnamon, nutmeg, and salt. Make a well in the center of the dry mixture. In a separate bowl, whisk the egg and sugar together. Stir in the buttermilk and oil. Pour liquid ingredients into the well in the dry mixture and stir just until moistened. Fold in the prunes or raisins. Spoon the batter into the prepared pan. Bake at 375 degrees F. for 40 minutes or until a toothpick inserted in the center of the loaf comes out clean. Let stand in pan for 10 minutes, then turn out onto wire rack to cool. Makes 1 loaf, about 16 slices.

NUTRITION (PER SLICE):		99 CALORIES
TOTAL FAT	2 g	(14% OF CALORIES)
PROTEIN	2 g	(10% OF CALORIES)
CARBOHYDRATES	19 g	(76% OF CALORIES)
CHOLESTEROL	14 mg	
SODIUM	83 mg	

Orange Nut Bread

1 orange
1 cup raisins
1 teaspoon vanilla
2 egg whites, beaten
2 cups flour
1 teaspoon baking powder
½ teaspoon baking soda
½ teaspoon salt
1 cup sugar
½ cup chopped walnuts

Spray an 8 x 4-inch loaf pan with nonstick cooking spray; set aside. Wash orange; squeeze juice. Pour juice into a 1-cup measure and add boiling water to make 1 full cup. Scrape the white part off the inside of the orange skin as much as possible. Chop orange rind and raisins very fine in food processor. (Raisins may be left whole if desired.) Combine vanilla, egg whites, and juice-water mixture; pour onto chopped fruits. Sift together the flour, baking powder, baking soda, and salt and add with sugar to fruit mixture. Stir in nuts. Pour into prepared loaf pan and bake at 350 degrees F. for 1 hour. Makes 1 loaf, about 12 slices.

NUTRITION (PER SLICE): 223 CALORIES

TOTAL FAT	3 g	(12% OF CALORIES)
PROTEIN	5 g	(9% OF CALORIES)
CARBOHYDRATES	44 g	(79% OF CALORIES)
CHOLESTEROL	0 mg	
SODIUM	183 mg	

Choco-Banana Almond Bread

2 or 3 medium-sized ripe bananas (1 cup mashed)
1½ cups flour
1 cup sugar
6 tablespoons unsweetened cocoa
1 teaspoon baking soda
½ teaspoon salt
¼ teaspoon baking powder
2 eggs
⅓ cup vegetable oil
⅓ cup chopped almonds

Preheat oven to 350 degrees F. Spray a 9 x 5-inch loaf pan with nonstick cooking spray; set aside. Mash bananas with fork and measure to make 1 cup. In a large bowl, mix together flour, sugar, cocoa, baking soda, salt, and baking powder. Make a well in the center of the dry ingredients. In a separate bowl, beat eggs, oil, and mashed bananas. Pour into well in dry mixture; mix just until moistened. Stir in almonds. Pour into prepared loaf pan. Bake for 55 to 60 minutes, or until wooden toothpick inserted in center comes out clean. Let stand in pan for 10 minutes, then turn out onto wire rack to cool. Makes 1 loaf, about 16 slices.

NUTRITION (PER SLICE): 182 CALORIES

TOTAL FAT	7 g	(35% OF CALORIES)
PROTEIN	3 g	(7% OF CALORIES)
CARBOHYDRATES	26 g	(58% OF CALORIES)
CHOLESTEROL	27 mg	
SODIUM	154 mg	

Cream Cheese Biscuits

2 cups flour
2½ teaspoons baking powder
½ teaspoon salt
¼ teaspoon baking soda
3 tablespoons light soft cream cheese (in tub)
2 tablespoons light margarine
½ cup skim milk

Spray a baking sheet with nonstick cooking spray; set aside. Combine flour, baking powder, salt, and baking soda in a large bowl. Cut in cream cheese and margarine with fork or pastry blender until mixture is the consistency of coarse meal. Add milk and stir into a firm dough. Place the dough on a lightly floured surface and knead a few times to make it smooth; then roll it out about ½-inch thick. Cut with biscuit cutter dipped in flour. Place biscuits on the prepared baking sheet; brush with milk, if desired. Bake at 425 degrees F. for 12 minutes or until the biscuits are light brown. Makes 12 biscuits.

NUTRITION (PER SERVING): 98 CALORIES

TOTAL FAT	2 g	(18% OF CALORIES)
PROTEIN	3 g	(12% OF CALORIES)
CARBOHYDRATES	17 g	(70% OF CALORIES)
CHOLESTEROL	2 mg	
SODIUM	230 mg	

Buttermilk Scones

2 tablespoons light margarine
1½ cups flour
½ cup stone-ground cornmeal
2 tablespoons sugar
1 teaspoon baking powder
1 teaspoon baking soda
¼ teaspoon salt
¼ cup golden raisins
¾ cup nonfat buttermilk

Preheat oven to 375 degrees F. Spray a baking sheet with nonstick cooking spray; set aside. Cut margarine into small pieces and place in refrigerator to chill. In a large bowl, stir together flour, cornmeal, sugar, baking powder, baking soda, and salt. Cut in chilled margarine with a pastry blender until mixture is the consistency of coarse meal. Stir in raisins. Make a well in the dry ingredients and pour buttermilk into it, stirring just until moistened. Place dough on a lightly floured surface and knead a few times to make it smooth. Roll dough into an 8-inch circle and cut into 10 wedges. Arrange wedges ¼ inch apart on the prepared baking sheet and bake for 20 to 22 minutes or until golden brown. Makes 10 scones.

NUTRITION (PER SERVING): 134 CALORIES

TOTAL FAT	2 g	(13% OF CALORIES)
PROTEIN	3 g	(9% OF CALORIES)
CARBOHYDRATES	26 g	(78% OF CALORIES)
CHOLESTEROL	1 mg	
SODIUM	263 mg	

Oat and Applesauce Pancakes

1 cup quick-cooking rolled oats
¼ cup whole wheat flour
¼ cup white flour
1 tablespoon baking powder
1 cup skim milk
2 tablespoons applesauce
4 egg whites

Stir together the oats, flours, and baking powder. Mix in milk and applesauce; blend well. Beat egg whites until soft peaks form; fold into batter. Spray a 12-inch skillet with nonstick cooking spray and place on stove over medium heat. Pour about ¼ cup of batter per pancake; cook until surface is covered with bubbles, about 1 to 2 minutes. Turn and brown 1 to 2 minutes more. Makes 10 pancakes.

NUTRITION (PER PANCAKE): 45 CALORIES

TOTAL FAT	0 g	(3% OF CALORIES)
PROTEIN	3 g	(30% OF CALORIES)
CARBOHYDRATES	7 g	(67% OF CALORIES)
CHOLESTEROL	1 mg	
SODIUM	140 mg	

Apple Pancakes

1½ cups flour
5 tablespoons instant nonfat dry milk
3½ tablespoons sugar
2¼ teaspoons baking powder
1 teaspoon cinnamon
1½ tablespoons margarine
1 egg, separated
1¼ cups skim milk
¼ cup sour cream
½ cup peeled, chopped apples

Thoroughly mix together flour, dry milk, sugar, baking powder, and cinnamon. Add margarine and blend with pastry blender until mixture is the consistency of coarse meal. Beat egg white until it stands in stiff, dry peaks. Set aside. Combine egg yolk, milk, and sour cream. Add to dry ingredients and stir just until moistened. Fold in the chopped apples. Gently fold in beaten egg whites, being careful to not overmix.

Spray a 12-inch skillet with nonstick cooking spray. Place on stove over medium heat. Pour about ¼ cup of batter per pancake; cook for 1 to 2 minutes or until surface of pancake is covered with bubbles. Turn and brown 1 to 2 minutes more. Makes 15 pancakes.

NUTRITION (PER PANCAKE): 87 CALORIES

TOTAL FAT	2 g	(23% OF CALORIES)
PROTEIN	3 g	(14% OF CALORIES)
CARBOHYDRATES	13 g	(63% OF CALORIES)
CHOLESTEROL	17 mg	
SODIUM	85 mg	

Super Hamburger Soup (page 34) and Old-Fashioned Corn Bread (page 20)

SOUPS AND STEWS

New England Clam Chowder

½ cup chopped onions
2 cups water
3 cups diced potatoes
2 cups finely chopped celery
8 cups skim milk
1 teaspoon chicken bouillon granules
4 cans (6½ ounces each) chopped clams, undrained
6 tablespoons cornstarch
½ cup water
4 tablespoons butter-flavored granules
1½ teaspoons salt
⅛ teaspoon pepper
1 dash garlic powder

On low heat in heavy 4-quart pan, cook onions in 2 cups water until soft but not brown (about 5 minutes). Add potatoes and celery. Cook until potatoes are tender, about 20 minutes. Add milk, bouillon, and clams with liquid. Heat through, stirring frequently to prevent burning. Blend cornstarch with ½ cup water until smooth; pour into chowder, stirring constantly over medium heat until thickened. Add butter-flavored granules, salt, pepper, and garlic powder. Taste to correct seasoning. Makes 12 servings.

NUTRITION (PER SERVING): 195 CALORIES

TOTAL FAT	1 g	(5% OF CALORIES)
PROTEIN	13 g	(26% OF CALORIES)
CARBOHYDRATES	33 g	(69% OF CALORIES)
CHOLESTEROL	19 mg	
SODIUM	486 mg	

Creamy Vegetable Soup

1 large carrot
1 large potato
1 medium onion
1 tablespoon butter or margarine
3 cloves garlic, crushed
1 bay leaf
¼ teaspoon thyme
2½ cups low-sodium chicken broth
2 cups 1% low-fat milk
⅛ teaspoon salt
⅛ teaspoon black pepper

Peel the carrot, potato, and onion and slice them thin. Melt butter or margarine in a heavy saucepan over low heat. Sauté carrots, onions, potatoes, garlic, bay leaf, and thyme in the butter for 1 minute. Stir in ½ cup of the chicken broth and cook, covered, until liquid has mostly evaporated, about 15 minutes.

Stir in the remaining 2 cups chicken broth and milk. Cook, uncovered, over medium heat, stirring occasionally, until vegetables are tender, about 30 minutes. Stir in salt and pepper. Makes 4 servings.

NUTRITION (PER SERVING): 220 CALORIES

TOTAL FAT	5 g	(20% OF CALORIES)
PROTEIN	9 g	(16% OF CALORIES)
CARBOHYDRATES	35 g	(64% OF CALORIES)
CHOLESTEROL	13 mg	
SODIUM	223 mg	

Classic French Onion Soup

½ tablespoon butter or margarine
4 medium onions, sliced
2 tablespoons flour
⅛ teaspoon sugar
5 cups low-sodium beef broth
½ teaspoon thyme
1 bay leaf
¼ teaspoon pepper
4 slices French bread, toasted
1 clove garlic, split lengthwise
2 tablespoons grated Parmesan cheese

Melt butter or margarine in a large heavy saucepan over medium heat. Stir in sliced onions and sauté until golden, about 8 to 10 minutes. Sprinkle with flour and sugar; cook 3 minutes longer, stirring constantly. Raise heat to medium high and add beef broth, thyme, bay leaf, and pepper. Bring to a boil, stirring constantly. Reduce heat and simmer, covered loosely, for 30 minutes. Remove and discard the bay leaf.

Preheat broiler. Rub the toasted pieces of French bread with the cut edge of the garlic clove and sprinkle with Parmesan cheese. Divide soup evenly among four individual bowls (make certain they are flameproof). Place a piece of bread, cheese side up, in each bowl. Set bowls under broiler, 4 to 6 inches from heat, and broil about 2 minutes or until cheese is golden brown. Makes 4 servings.

NUTRITION (PER SERVING): 203 CALORIES

TOTAL FAT	3 g	(13% OF CALORIES)
PROTEIN	19 g	(37% OF CALORIES)
CARBOHYDRATES	25 g	(50% OF CALORIES)
CHOLESTEROL	6 mg	
SODIUM	301 mg	

Chicken Corn Chowder

2 slices bacon
¼ cup chopped onions
3 tablespoons water
2 cups low-sodium chicken broth
1 package (10 ounces) frozen corn
2 potatoes, peeled and chopped
½ cup chopped celery
½ teaspoon salt
¼ teaspoon pepper
2 tablespoons flour
2 cups skim milk
2 cups cooked chicken or turkey (light meat), chopped

Cook bacon till crisp in a large heavy saucepan. Drain bacon, wiping drippings from saucepan with a paper towel. Crumble bacon and set it aside.

In same saucepan, cook onions in 3 tablespoons water until tender. Add chicken broth, frozen corn, potatoes, celery, salt, and pepper. Bring to a boil. Reduce heat; cover and simmer until vegetables are tender, about 15 minutes.

Stir flour into milk until smooth. Pour into vegetable mixture and cook, stirring constantly, until thickened. Add chopped chicken or turkey and stir over heat 2 or 3 minutes more, until heated through. Top with crumbled bacon. Makes 6 servings.

NUTRITION (PER SERVING): 235 CALORIES

TOTAL FAT	3 g	(11% OF CALORIES)
PROTEIN	28 g	(48% OF CALORIES)
CARBOHYDRATES	24 g	(41% OF CALORIES)
CHOLESTEROL	50 mg	
SODIUM	515 mg	

Black Bean Soup

1 tablespoon vegetable oil
1 cup chopped onions
2 cloves garlic, minced
2 cans (15 ounces each) black beans, drained
½ cup water
1½ teaspoons cumin
1 drop hot pepper sauce
1 can (14½ ounces) chopped
   stewed tomatoes, undrained
1 can (10½ ounces) low-sodium chicken broth
1 can (4 ounces) chopped mild
   green chilies, undrained
1 tablespoon lemon juice
¼ cup low-fat plain yogurt

In a large heavy saucepan over medium heat, sauté onions and garlic in vegetable oil until translucent. Add 1 cup of the beans and mash with a potato masher. Stir in remaining beans, water, cumin, hot pepper sauce, tomatoes with liquid, chicken broth, and chilies with liquid. Bring mixture to a boil. Reduce heat; cover and simmer for 15 minutes to blend flavors. Remove soup from heat and add the lemon juice. Ladle into bowls and top each with a dollop of yogurt. Makes 4 servings.

NUTRITION (PER SERVING): 399 CALORIES

TOTAL FAT	5 g	(12% OF CALORIES)
PROTEIN	22 g	(22% OF CALORIES)
CARBOHYDRATES	65 g	(65% OF CALORIES)
CHOLESTEROL	1 mg	
SODIUM	441 mg	

Beef and Barley Soup

½ pound lean boneless round steak
8 cups water
1 can (14½ ounces) chopped
   stewed tomatoes, undrained
1 can (10½) ounces beef broth
½ cup chopped onions
1 clove garlic, minced
½ teaspoon basil
¼ teaspoon salt
2 bay leaves
½ cup barley
1 cup water
1 package (10 ounces) frozen mixed vegetables

Prepare steak by trimming fat and cutting into 1-inch cubes. In a large pot (at least 4-quart capacity) stir together 8 cups water, steak cubes, tomatoes with liquid, beef broth, onions, garlic, basil, salt, and bay leaves. Bring to a boil. Reduce heat; cover and simmer for 1 hour.

Place barley in a strainer and run cold water over it to rinse. Gradually add barley, along with 1 cup water, to soup in pot; cover and simmer again for 1 hour. With a metal spoon, skim fat from top of soup. Add frozen vegetables to pot; cover and simmer a third time until meat and vegetables are tender, about 30 to 40 minutes. Remove and discard bay leaves. Makes 10 servings.

NUTRITION (PER SERVING): 120 CALORIES

TOTAL FAT	4 g	(30% OF CALORIES)
PROTEIN	8 g	(27% OF CALORIES)
CARBOHYDRATES	13 g	(43% OF CALORIES)
CHOLESTEROL	15 mg	
SODIUM	353 mg	

Italian Vegetable Soup

6 ounces Italian sausage
2 cans (14½ ounces each) stewed
    tomatoes, undrained
2 cups low-sodium beef broth
1 package (10 ounces) frozen mixed vegetables
½ teaspoon salt
½ teaspoon garlic powder
¾ cup uncooked small seashell pasta

In a large saucepan over medium heat, brown sausage, cooking and stirring until crumbly. Drain sausage and wipe drippings from pan with a paper towel. Return sausage to pan and stir in tomatoes with liquid, beef broth, frozen vegetables, salt, and garlic powder. Bring to a boil. Cover, reduce heat to medium low, and cook 5 minutes. Stir in pasta shells; cover and cook an additional 10 minutes or until pasta is tender. Makes 8 servings.

NUTRITION (PER SERVING): 172 CALORIES

TOTAL FAT	8 g	(42% OF CALORIES)
PROTEIN	9 g	(21% OF CALORIES)
CARBOHYDRATES	16 g	(37% OF CALORIES)
CHOLESTEROL	16 mg	
SODIUM	550 mg	

Potato Corn Chowder

¼ cup finely chopped celery
¼ cup finely chopped onions
2 cups low-sodium chicken broth
1 cup water
⅛ teaspoon pepper
1 cup dehydrated mashed potato flakes
1¼ cups canned cream-style corn
1½ cups 1% low-fat milk
¾ cup grated reduced-fat
    sharp cheddar cheese
1 tablespoon lemon juice

Spray a large saucepan with nonstick cooking spray; preheat briefly on stove. Add celery and onions and sauté for 3 minutes or until tender. Add chicken broth, water, and pepper. Bring to a boil and remove from heat. Stir in potato flakes until moistened; then add corn. Stir in milk and cheese. Cook for 5 minutes over medium heat or until cheese melts. Stir in lemon juice. Garnish with freshly ground pepper, if desired. Makes 6 servings.

NUTRITION (PER SERVING): 201 CALORIES

TOTAL FAT	4 g	(18% OF CALORIES)
PROTEIN	10 g	(21% OF CALORIES)
CARBOHYDRATES	31 g	(61% OF CALORIES)
CHOLESTEROL	10 mg	
SODIUM	292 mg	

Potato Soup

1½ cups sliced leeks or green onions
¼ cup water
5 cups cubed potatoes
¾ cup chopped celery
1⅓ cups cubed carrots
1 teaspoon salt
2 cups water
¼ cup butter or margarine
¼ cup flour
¼ teaspoon pepper
1 teaspoon salt
4 cups skim milk
2 cubes chicken bouillon

Sauté leeks or green onions in ¼ cup water in a large kettle until tender. Add potatoes, celery, carrots, 1 teaspoon salt, and 2 cups water. Cover and simmer for 20 to 25 minutes or until vegetables are tender.

Meanwhile, melt butter or margarine in a medium saucepan. Add flour, pepper, and 1 teaspoon salt. Cook until smooth and bubbly. Gradually add milk and bouillon. Cook and stir until mixture thickens. Stir into vegetables. Simmer, stirring occasionally, until heated through. Makes 8 servings.

NUTRITION (PER SERVING): 231 CALORIES

TOTAL FAT	6 g	(25% OF CALORIES)
PROTEIN	8 g	(13% OF CALORIES)
CARBOHYDRATES	35 g	(62% OF CALORIES)
CHOLESTEROL	18 mg	
SODIUM	1014 mg	

Peasant Soup

1 pound dried Great Northern beans
6 cups water
1 can (14½ ounces) chopped stewed
    tomatoes, undrained
3 carrots, sliced
3 stalks celery, sliced
2 onions, chopped
2 cloves garlic, minced
1½ teaspoons salt
1 teaspoon basil
½ teaspoon pepper
2 bay leaves
2 tablespoons olive oil

Place beans in a large saucepan and cover with boiling water. Cover and let stand 1 hour. Drain beans and rinse them in a strainer under running water. In a large pot, stir together beans, 6 cups water, tomatoes with liquid, carrots, celery, onions, garlic, salt, basil, pepper, and bay leaves. Bring to a boil. Reduce heat and simmer, covered, for 1½ hours or until beans are tender. Remove and discard bay leaves. Add oil and cook 1 to 2 minutes longer, or until heated through. Makes 12 servings.

NUTRITION (PER SERVING): 179 CALORIES

TOTAL FAT	3 g	(15% OF CALORIES)
PROTEIN	9 g	(20% OF CALORIES)
CARBOHYDRATES	29 g	(65% OF CALORIES)
CHOLESTEROL	0 mg	
SODIUM	421 mg	

Split Pea Soup

2 cups dried split peas (about 1 pound)
8 cups water
1 cup chopped onions
1 cup extra-lean ham, chopped in small pieces
1 tablespoon salt
¼ teaspoon pepper
4 tablespoons cornstarch
½ cup cold water

Combine split peas, water, onions, ham, salt, and pepper in a large soup kettle. Simmer for 1½ to 2 hours, or longer if desired. (Soup will be thicker the longer it cooks.) Blend cornstarch in cold water until smooth; stir into hot soup to thicken. Makes 10 servings.

NUTRITION (PER SERVING): 176 CALORIES

TOTAL FAT	1 g	(6% OF CALORIES)
PROTEIN	13 g	(29% OF CALORIES)
CARBOHYDRATES	28 g	(64% OF CALORIES)
CHOLESTEROL	7 mg	
SODIUM	878 mg	

Super Hamburger Soup

Pictured on page 27.

1½ pounds extra-lean ground beef
2 onions, chopped
4 stalks celery, chopped
1 green bell pepper, chopped
2 cans (14½ ounces each) chopped stewed tomatoes, undrained
1 can (6 ounces) tomato paste
4 cups water
4 medium carrots, sliced
2 large potatoes, diced
1 can (16 ounces) corn, undrained
1 can (15 ounces) red kidney beans, undrained
1 can (15 ounces) baby lima beans or garbanzos, undrained
1½ teaspoons salt
½ teaspoon pepper
2 zucchini, sliced

Cook ground beef, onions, celery, and green pepper in a large pot until meat is brown and crumbly and onion is translucent. Drain. Add tomatoes with liquid, tomato paste, water, carrots, potatoes, corn, kidney beans, lima beans or garbanzos, salt, and pepper. Bring to a boil; reduce heat and simmer, covered, about 20 minutes. Add zucchini and cook another 10 to 15 minutes or until vegetables are tender. Makes 12 servings.

Note: Experiment with herbs such as basil, marjoram, thyme, and bay leaves for a more flavorful broth.

NUTRITION (PER SERVING): 285 CALORIES

TOTAL FAT	6 g	(19% OF CALORIES)
PROTEIN	16 g	(22% OF CALORIES)
CARBOHYDRATES	43 g	(59% OF CALORIES)
CHOLESTEROL	20 mg	
SODIUM	494 mg	

Vegetable Beef Soup

6 cups water
1 cup diced tomatoes
1½ cups diced carrots
1 cup diced celery
¼ cup chopped onions
1 cube beef bouillon
½ cup green beans
1 cup cooked and diced potatoes
1½ cups (about ½ pound) stew meat,
   cooked and cut in bite-size pieces
1 cup water
1 cup peas
Salt and pepper to taste

In 6 cups water, cook tomatoes, carrots, celery, onions, and beef bouillon until carrots and celery are tender. Add beans, potatoes, stew meat, and additional 1 cup water. Simmer, covered, until vegetables are tender. Add peas about 5 minutes before serving. Add salt and pepper to taste. Makes 12 servings.

NUTRITION (PER SERVING): 62 CALORIES

TOTAL FAT	1 g	(12% OF CALORIES)
PROTEIN	6 g	(37% OF CALORIES)
CARBOHYDRATES	8 g	(51% OF CALORIES)
CHOLESTEROL	11 mg	
SODIUM	99 mg	

Vegetarian Chili

1 cup chopped onions
3 cloves garlic, minced
1 cup water
½ cup diced green bell peppers
2 cans (14½ ounces each) chopped
   stewed tomatoes, undrained
1 can (15 ounces) red kidney beans, drained
1 can (15 ounces) garbanzo beans, drained
2 tablespoons chili powder
1½ teaspoons cumin
¼ cup low-fat sour cream

Spray a large pot with nonstick cooking spray and preheat it on the stove. Sauté onions and garlic in heated pot over medium heat for 5 minutes. Stir in water, green peppers, tomatoes with liquid, kidney beans, garbanzo beans, chili powder, and cumin. Bring to a boil. Reduce heat and simmer, uncovered, for 30 minutes to blend flavors and thicken chili. Dish into individual bowls and top each with a dollop of low-fat sour cream. Makes 4 servings.

NUTRITION (PER SERVING): 395 CALORIES

TOTAL FAT	5 g	(12% OF CALORIES)
PROTEIN	19 g	(19% OF CALORIES)
CARBOHYDRATES	68 g	(69% OF CALORIES)
CHOLESTEROL	2 mg	
SODIUM	442 mg	

Lentil Stew

1 cup dried lentils
4 cups low-sodium beef broth
2 cans (14½ ounces each) chopped
    stewed tomatoes, undrained
1 medium onion, chopped
2 stalks celery, diced
2 cloves garlic, minced
1 teaspoon rosemary
¼ teaspoon pepper
4 carrots, peeled and cubed, divided
2 tablespoons light margarine
8 small white boiling onions, peeled
¼ pound small fresh mushrooms, halved
4 potatoes (about 1 pound), peeled and cubed

Rinse and sort the lentils and combine them in a large soup kettle with the beef broth, tomatoes with liquid, chopped onions, celery, garlic, rosemary, pepper, and half of the carrots. Bring mixture just to simmering point over medium heat. Reduce heat; cover and simmer gently for 30 to 35 minutes.

While mixture is simmering, melt margarine in a large heavy skillet. Sauté the remaining carrots along with the small white onions in the margarine until lightly browned, about 5 to 7 minutes. Stir in the mushrooms and cook an additional 2 or 3 minutes, stirring constantly. Add potatoes and sautéed vegetables to soup in kettle. Cover and simmer an additional 20 to 25 minutes or until potatoes and lentils are tender. Makes 8 servings.

NUTRITION (PER SERVING): 251 CALORIES

TOTAL FAT	3 g	(11% OF CALORIES)
PROTEIN	16 g	(17% OF CALORIES)
CARBOHYDRATES	40 g	(72% OF CALORIES)
CHOLESTEROL	0 mg	
SODIUM	565 mg	

Hearty Beef Stew

1½ pounds lean boneless round steak
1 can (14½ ounces) chopped stewed
    tomatoes, undrained
3 cups water
1 medium onion, sliced thin
1 clove garlic, minced
1 teaspoon salt
¼ teaspoon pepper
1 bay leaf
1 tablespoon lemon juice
1 teaspoon Worcestershire sauce
6 carrots, cubed
4 potatoes, cubed
½ cup sliced celery
½ cup water
¼ cup flour

Prepare steak by trimming visible fat and cutting meat into 1-inch cubes. Coat a large pot with nonstick cooking spray and brown meat in pot over low heat. Add tomatoes with liquid, water, onions, garlic, salt, pepper, bay leaf, lemon juice, and Worcestershire sauce. Heat just to simmering point; reduce heat, cover, and simmer for 2 hours, stirring occasionally to prevent meat from sticking to bottom. Add carrots, potatoes, and celery and cook, covered, an additional 30 to 35 minutes, until meat and vegetables are tender. Blend ½ cup water with flour until smooth; pour gradually into stew and cook, stirring, until thickened, about 5 minutes. Remove and discard bay leaf. Makes 8 servings.

NUTRITION (PER SERVING): 243 CALORIES

TOTAL FAT	2 g	(7% OF CALORIES)
PROTEIN	26 g	(48% OF CALORIES)
CARBOHYDRATES	25 g	(45% OF CALORIES)
CHOLESTEROL	67 mg	
SODIUM	434 mg	

Wonton Soup

Wontons

½ pound lean ground pork
¼ cup minced onions
¼ cup minced celery
1 tablespoon soy sauce
1 egg
½ teaspoon cornstarch
24 wonton wrappers
2 quarts water

Keep wonton wrappers covered with a damp dish towel while you are working to prevent them from drying out.

Combine pork, onions, celery, soy sauce, egg, and cornstarch in a large bowl. Mix well. Dampen one side of a wonton wrapper with water. Place wonton wrapper with 1 corner facing you. Place 1 level teaspoon of filling in center of wrapper. Fold wrapper in half to form a triangle, with the point facing away from you. Press wrapper firmly closed around the filling. Fold left and right sides of triangle up so that left and right points meet top point of triangle. Moisten and seal around edges. Repeat with remaining wonton wrappers and filling.

In a large saucepan, bring to a boil 2 quarts of water. Carefully drop wontons into boiling water. Bring to a boil again and cook 8 minutes. With a slotted spoon, remove wontons from water and drain. Wontons are now ready to be added to Wonton Soup.

Soup

6 cups low-sodium chicken broth
½ teaspoon salt
¼ teaspoon white pepper
1½ cups thinly sliced fresh mushrooms
¼ pound fresh spinach
24 cooked wontons
½ cup finely chopped green onions

In a large saucepan, combine chicken broth, salt, pepper, and mushrooms. Bring to a boil, cover, and simmer 5 minutes. Thoroughly wash spinach, trim, and shred into small pieces. Add spinach and cooked wontons to broth and bring to a boil again. Simmer for 5 minutes more. Ladle into soup bowls and top with chopped green onions. Serve immediately. Makes 12 servings.

NUTRITION (PER SERVING): 109 CALORIES

TOTAL FAT	3 g	(16% OF CALORIES)
PROTEIN	9 g	(24% OF CALORIES)
CARBOHYDRATES	12 g	(61% OF CALORIES)
CHOLESTEROL	42 mg	
SODIUM	352 mg	

MEATS

Slow-Cooked Swiss Steak

2 tablespoons vegetable oil

1½ pounds boneless beef top round steak,
  cut into 8 serving portions

¼ cup flour

1 can (14½ ounces) chopped stewed
  tomatoes, undrained

1 can (8 ounces) tomato sauce

1 cup chopped onions

1 clove garlic, minced

1 teaspoon sugar

½ teaspoon salt

¼ teaspoon pepper

½ cup cold water

1 tablespoon cornstarch

Heat oil in a large frying pan. Dredge beef pieces in flour and brown slowly in oil. Place browned meat in a slow cooker. Combine tomatoes with liquid, tomato sauce, onions, garlic, sugar, salt, and pepper, and pour over beef. Cover and cook on low setting for 5 to 6 hours or until meat is tender. Blend the cold water and cornstarch until smooth; stir into liquid in slow cooker and cook on high setting, stirring constantly, until thickened. Makes 8 servings.

NUTRITION (PER SERVING): 177 CALORIES

TOTAL FAT	7 g	(33% OF CALORIES)
PROTEIN	21 g	(47% OF CALORIES)
CARBOHYDRATES	9 g	(20% OF CALORIES)
CHOLESTEROL	49 mg	
SODIUM	712 mg	

Stir-Fried Beef and Peppers

3 tablespoons soy sauce

1 tablespoon lemon juice

4 teaspoons cornstarch

¼ teaspoon sugar

⅛ teaspoon ginger

1 pound boneless beef top round steak,
  cut in paper-thin strips (easier to cut
  if partially frozen)

¼ cup olive oil, divided

½ pound (about 3 cups) thickly sliced mushrooms

2 onions, quartered

1 green bell pepper, cut in squares or strips

½ teaspoon salt

Combine soy sauce, lemon juice, cornstarch, sugar, and ginger. Pour over meat strips; let stand while preparing vegetables.

Heat 2 tablespoons of the olive oil in a large frying pan. Add mushrooms, onions, green peppers, and salt and stir-fry until vegetables are tender-crisp, about 5 minutes. Lift vegetables from the oil and set aside. Add the remaining oil to the frying pan, heat, and add meat with marinade. Stir-fry meat in the hot oil 1 to 2 minutes, until it loses its pink color. Add vegetables and stir until hot. Makes 6 servings.

NUTRITION (PER SERVING): 258 CALORIES

TOTAL FAT	12 g	(42% OF CALORIES)
PROTEIN	26 g	(41% OF CALORIES)
CARBOHYDRATES	11 g	(17% OF CALORIES)
CHOLESTEROL	64 mg	
SODIUM	760 mg	

Yankee Pot Roast

1½ pounds boneless beef round roast
¼ teaspoon pepper
1½ cups low-sodium beef broth
½ cup water
1 can (8 ounces) tomato sauce
2 medium onions, sliced thin
2 cloves garlic, minced
½ teaspoon thyme
½ teaspoon marjoram
½ teaspoon basil
¼ pound fresh mushrooms, sliced thin
1 tablespoon minced fresh parsley

Sprinkle the pepper over the roast and rub into meat. Brown roast in broiler, about 4 inches from heat, about 10 minutes, or until browned on all sides. In a large, heavy pot (4-quart capacity) mix together the beef broth, water, tomato sauce, onions, garlic, thyme, marjoram, and basil. Place the browned roast in the pot and bring ingredients just to a simmer over medium heat. Cover tightly and place in oven heated to 325 degrees F. Cook for 2 to 2½ hours, or until roast is tender.

Make a sauce for the pot roast by pureeing the onions and liquid from the pot in a food processor or blender. Sauté the mushrooms in a skillet sprayed with nonstick cooking spray; add pureed mixture and heat through. Spoon sauce over sliced pot roast and sprinkle with parsley, if desired. Makes 6 servings.

NUTRITION (PER SERVING): 196 CALORIES

TOTAL FAT	5 g	(21% OF CALORIES)
PROTEIN	27 g	(56% OF CALORIES)
CARBOHYDRATES	11 g	(23% OF CALORIES)
CHOLESTEROL	59 mg	
SODIUM	307 mg	

Taco-Stuffed Green Peppers

1 pound extra-lean ground beef
1 package taco seasoning mix
¾ cup water
1 small can (8 ounces) kidney beans, rinsed and drained
1 cup salsa
2 quarts water
4 medium green bell peppers
1 tomato, chopped
½ cup shredded reduced-fat cheddar cheese
½ cup nonfat sour cream

Preheat oven to 350 degrees F. Brown the ground beef in a large skillet; drain. Add the taco seasoning, ¾ cup water, kidney beans, and salsa; stir to mix well. Bring to a boil over medium-high heat. Reduce heat and simmer, uncovered, for 5 minutes to blend flavors.

Heat 2 quarts water to boiling in a large saucepan. Cut peppers in half lengthwise and remove seeds. Place pepper halves in boiling water; cook for 3 minutes, then remove and drain. Arrange the pepper halves in an ungreased 13 x 9-inch baking dish. Divide the ground beef mixture among the halves (about ½ cup in each). Cover dish with aluminum foil and bake for 15 to 20 minutes or until the peppers are tender but still crisp and the filling is heated through. Top each serving with chopped tomatoes, cheese, and sour cream. Makes 8 servings.

NUTRITION (PER SERVING): 213 CALORIES

TOTAL FAT	5 g	(21% OF CALORIES)
PROTEIN	20 g	(38% OF CALORIES)
CARBOHYDRATES	22 g	(41% OF CALORIES)
CHOLESTEROL	47 mg	
SODIUM	286 mg	

Pot Roast Dinner

2 tablespoons olive oil
2 pounds boneless beef round roast
1 can (10½ ounces) reduced-fat
   cream of mushroom soup
1 envelope onion soup mix
1 cup water
6 medium potatoes, quartered
6 carrots, cut in chunks
2 tablespoons flour
¼ cup water

Heat oil in a large heavy pot (6-quart capacity). Add roast and cook over medium heat, turning occasionally, until browned on all sides. Spoon off fat. Reduce heat to low. Combine mushroom soup, onion soup mix, and 1 cup water; pour over roast. Cover and simmer over low heat for 2 hours or until roast is tender. Add potatoes and carrots, cover, and cook an additional 40 minutes or until vegetables are tender. Remove roast and vegetables to a serving platter.

Raise heat to medium and cook the pan liquid, uncovered, until slightly thick. Blend flour and ¼ cup water until smooth. Gradually stir flour mixture into liquid in pot. Cook, stirring constantly, until mixture bubbles and thickens. Serve with roast. Makes 8 servings.

NUTRITION (PER SERVING): 334 CALORIES

TOTAL FAT	14 g	(38% OF CALORIES)
PROTEIN	25 g	(30% OF CALORIES)
CARBOHYDRATES	27 g	(32% OF CALORIES)
CHOLESTEROL	66 mg	
SODIUM	686 mg	

Lion House Meat Loaf

½ cup chopped onions
1 can (10½ ounces) tomato soup
¼ cup water
1 teaspoon Worcestershire sauce
1 dash pepper
2 pounds extra-lean ground beef
1 teaspoon salt
2 eggs, lightly beaten

Make sauce: Spray a frying pan with nonstick cooking spray and preheat briefly on stove. Add onions and sauté until tender. Stir in tomato soup, water, Worcestershire sauce, and pepper; simmer a few minutes to blend flavors.

Make meat loaf: Mix ground beef, salt, eggs, and half the sauce until well blended. Mold into a 9 x 5-inch loaf pan. Bake at 350 degrees for 1½ hours. Remove from oven and allow to stand for about 10 minutes. Serve with remaining sauce. Makes 10 servings.

NUTRITION (PER SERVING): 160 CALORIES

TOTAL FAT	8 g	(45% OF CALORIES)
PROTEIN	19 g	(47% OF CALORIES)
CARBOHYDRATES	3 g	(8% OF CALORIES)
CHOLESTEROL	105 mg	
SODIUM	434 mg	

Marinated Steak and Onions

1 cup water
¼ cup low-sodium Worcestershire sauce
1 teaspoon beef bouillon granules
¼ teaspoon nutmeg
¼ teaspoon red pepper
⅛ teaspoon allspice
1 bay leaf
2 pounds boneless beef round tip steaks
2 large sweet onions

Mix together the water, Worcestershire sauce, bouillon, nutmeg, red pepper, allspice, and bay leaf. Trim fat from steaks and cut into serving-size portions. Place in shallow baking dish. Cut onions in ¼-inch slices and separate into rings. Arrange over steak in dish. Pour marinade over top. Cover and refrigerate at least 8 hours or overnight, turning steaks occasionally.

Spray the rack of a broiler pan with nonstick cooking spray. Remove steak from marinade, reserving remaining ingredients. Place steak on rack of broiler pan and broil 5 to 6 inches from heat to desired degree of doneness. (For medium steaks, broil 7 to 8 minutes on each side.) Meanwhile, spray a large skillet with nonstick cooking spray and preheat briefly on stove. Remove onion rings from marinade and sauté over medium-high heat until tender-crisp. Pour reserved marinade over onions and heat to simmering; cover, reduce heat, and simmer 4 to 6 minutes or until onion is tender. Remove and discard bay leaf. Spoon onions and marinade over cooked steaks. Makes 8 servings.

NUTRITION (PER SERVING): 180 CALORIES

TOTAL FAT	6 g	(31% OF CALORIES)
PROTEIN	25 g	(56% OF CALORIES)
CARBOHYDRATES	6 g	(13% OF CALORIES)
CHOLESTEROL	69 mg	
SODIUM	86 mg	

Meatball Cassoulet

1¼ cups dry navy beans, sorted and rinsed
4 cups water
½ pound extra-lean ground beef
1 tablespoon Worcestershire sauce
¼ teaspoon salt
3 cups water
½ cup chopped onions
½ cup chopped celery
1 clove garlic, minced
1 tablespoon Worcestershire sauce
¾ teaspoon salt
½ teaspoon basil
½ teaspoon oregano
½ teaspoon paprika
1 can (14½ ounces) chopped stewed
   tomatoes, undrained
1 can (8 ounces) tomato sauce
1 can (4 ounces) chopped green chilies, undrained
1 carrot, scraped and grated
3 cups hot cooked rice

Soak beans in 4 cups water for 8 hours. Drain water and place beans in a large heavy pot. In a small bowl, mix ground beef, 1 tablespoon Worcestershire sauce, and ¼ teaspoon salt; mold into 18 small meatballs. Cook meatballs in a nonstick frying pan over medium heat, turning to brown evenly. Add meatballs to beans in pot.

Pour 3 cups water over meatballs and beans. Stir in onions, celery, garlic, 1 tablespoon Worcestershire sauce, ¾ teaspoon salt, basil, oregano, and paprika. Cover and bring to a boil; reduce heat and simmer for 1½ hours or until beans are tender. Add tomatoes with liquid, tomato sauce, chilies with liquid, and grated carrot. Cover and simmer 10 minutes more. Spoon into individual bowls and top each with ½ cup hot rice. Makes 6 servings.

NUTRITION (PER SERVING): 210 CALORIES

TOTAL FAT	3 g	(14% OF CALORIES)
PROTEIN	15 g	(22% OF CALORIES)
CARBOHYDRATES	32 g	(64% OF CALORIES)
CHOLESTEROL	32 mg	
SODIUM	802 mg	

Grilled Steak with Italian Vegetables

1 pound boneless beef top sirloin steak,
    cut 1 inch thick
1 teaspoon whole black peppercorns,
    coarsely cracked
1 tablespoon butter or margarine
4 green onions, sliced diagonally
    into 1-inch pieces
3 small zucchini, cut into strips
1 small green bell pepper, cut into strips
1 clove garlic, minced
½ teaspoon oregano
12 cherry tomatoes, halved

Trim excess fat from steak. Rub the cracked pepper into the steak evenly on both sides. To grill on barbecue, place steak over medium-hot coals and grill 15 to 20 minutes or to desired degree of doneness, turning once during cooking time. Or, if you prefer, place steak on rack of broiler pan and cook in broiler, 3 inches from heat, for 8 to 15 minutes.

While steak is cooking, melt butter or margarine in a medium skillet. Stir in green onions, zucchini and bell pepper strips, garlic, and oregano. Stir-fry the vegetables over medium heat for 4 minutes. Add the cherry tomato halves, cover, and cook an additional 1 minute. Place vegetables on serving platter. Slice meat diagonally across the grain and arrange on platter with the vegetables. Serve immediately. Makes 4 servings.

NUTRITION (PER SERVING): 213 CALORIES

TOTAL FAT	9 g	(39% OF CALORIES)
PROTEIN	27 g	(52% OF CALORIES)
CARBOHYDRATES	5 g	(9% OF CALORIES)
CHOLESTEROL	83 mg	
SODIUM	90 mg	

Stove-Top Beef Casserole

¾ pound extra-lean ground beef
1 cup chopped onions
½ cup chopped green bell peppers
2 cans (8 ounces each) tomato sauce
2 cups water
¾ cup uncooked brown rice
2 teaspoons chili powder
½ teaspoon salt
¼ teaspoon pepper
1 can (15 ounces) corn, undrained

In a large frying pan, cook ground beef with onions and bell peppers, stirring until meat is crumbly and browned and vegetables are tender. Drain and place in a large heavy pot. Add tomato sauce and water. Bring to a boil over medium-high heat and stir in uncooked rice, chili powder, salt, and pepper. Reduce heat, cover, and simmer 50 minutes. Stir in corn with liquid, adding a little additional water if necessary. Cover and cook 10 minutes more, or until rice is done. Makes 6 servings.

NUTRITION (PER SERVING): 232 CALORIES

TOTAL FAT	4 g	(31% OF CALORIES)
PROTEIN	19 g	(27% OF CALORIES)
CARBOHYDRATES	30 g	(42% OF CALORIES)
CHOLESTEROL	48 mg	
SODIUM	762 mg	

Beef Stroganoff

1 clove garlic, cut in quarters
2 tablespoons olive oil
1½ pounds lean boneless beef, cut into
    thin bite-size strips
½ cup chopped onions
½ cup chopped celery (optional)
¾ teaspoon salt
¼ teaspoon pepper
½ pound sliced fresh mushrooms
¼ cup flour
1½ cups skim milk
½ teaspoon paprika
1 cup light sour cream

Heat garlic in oil in heavy skillet for a few minutes, then remove and discard garlic. Add meat to skillet; brown slightly. Add onions, celery, salt, and pepper. Cover and cook slowly for 35 to 45 minutes or until meat is completely tender, stirring occasionally. Add water during cooking, if necessary. Add mushrooms. Cover and cook gently until mushrooms are tender, about 10 minutes.

With slotted spoon, remove the meat and mushrooms to top of double boiler. Blend flour into drippings in pan. Slowly stir in milk. Cook and stir over medium heat until mixture thickens. Sprinkle in paprika. Add sauce to the meat and mushroom mixture in double boiler. Stir in sour cream. Heat over boiling water until just heated through. Serve over rice or noodles. Makes 6 servings.

NUTRITION (PER SERVING): 263 CALORIES

TOTAL FAT	11 g	(38% OF CALORIES)
PROTEIN	30 g	(46% OF CALORIES)
CARBOHYDRATES	11 g	(16% OF CALORIES)
CHOLESTEROL	70 mg	
SODIUM	433 mg	

Spinach and Cheese Stuffed Meat Loaf

1½ pounds extra-lean ground beef
¾ cup soft bread crumbs
¼ cup liquid egg substitute
1 teaspoon salt
½ teaspoon onion powder
⅛ teaspoon pepper
1 package (10 ounces) frozen chopped spinach,
    thawed and well drained
¾ cup shredded part-skim mozzarella
    cheese, divided
3 tablespoons grated Parmesan cheese
1 teaspoon Italian seasoning
¼ teaspoon garlic powder
3 tablespoons ketchup

Combine ground beef, bread crumbs, egg substitute, salt, onion powder, and pepper, mixing well. On a length of waxed paper or aluminum foil, pat meat mixture into a 10 x 14-inch rectangle. Mix together the spinach, ½ cup mozzarella cheese, Parmesan cheese, Italian seasoning, and garlic powder. Spread this mixture over the meat rectangle to within ¾ inch of edges all around. Starting at the short end, roll the meat up as you would a jelly roll. Seal meat over filling on ends. Place roll, seam side down, on a rack in a shallow pan. Bake, uncovered, at 350 degrees F. for 1 hour. Spread ketchup over top of meat loaf and bake an additional 15 minutes. Sprinkle with ¼ cup mozzarella cheese. Let stand 10 minutes to melt cheese and make loaf easier to slice. Makes 6 servings.

NUTRITION (PER SERVING): 259 CALORIES

TOTAL FAT	9 g	(31% OF CALORIES)
PROTEIN	30 g	(43% OF CALORIES)
CARBOHYDRATES	14 g	(26% OF CALORIES)
CHOLESTEROL	88 mg	
SODIUM	776 mg	

Garden Chicken Salad (page 56) and Soft Bread Sticks (page 17)

Teriyaki Kabobs

2 pounds boneless beef top sirloin
½ cup ketchup
½ cup sugar
½ cup soy sauce
1 teaspoon garlic powder
1 teaspoon ginger
½ fresh pineapple, trimmed and cut into
   1-inch chunks
2 small zucchini, cut into 1-inch chunks
½ pound medium-size whole fresh mushrooms
½ pound small white boiling onions, peeled
1 green or red bell pepper, cut into 1-inch pieces

Trim any visible fat from meat and cut in 1½-inch cubes. Mix together the ketchup, sugar, soy sauce, garlic powder, and ginger. Place beef cubes in a baking dish and pour marinade over them. Cover dish and refrigerate at least 8 hours or overnight. Drain beef, reserving marinade. Thread meat chunks alternately with pineapple and vegetables on long skewers. Grill over hot coals, turning often, until meat reaches desired doneness and vegetables are tender, about 15 to 20 minutes. Meanwhile, place reserved marinade in a small saucepan and simmer it for 15 minutes over low heat. Serve with meat and vegetables. Makes 8 servings.

NUTRITION (PER SERVING): 296 CALORIES

TOTAL FAT	12 g	(36% OF CALORIES)
PROTEIN	24 g	(32% OF CALORIES)
CARBOHYDRATES	23 g	(32% OF CALORIES)
CHOLESTEROL	76 mg	
SODIUM	1175 mg	

Busy-Day Barbecued Beef

1¼ pounds lean stewing beef
1 bottle (18 ounces) barbecue sauce
8 hamburger buns

Place beef in slow cooker and fill ¾ full with water. Cook on low setting for 8 to 9 hours or overnight. Drain beef and break apart with fork. Return beef to slow cooker and pour barbecue sauce over it. Cook on low setting an additional 45 minutes to 1 hour. Serve on buns. Makes 8 servings.

NUTRITION (PER SERVING, MEAT AND BUN): 290 CALORIES

TOTAL FAT	10 g	(31% OF CALORIES)
PROTEIN	22 g	(30% OF CALORIES)
CARBOHYDRATES	28 g	(39% OF CALORIES)
CHOLESTEROL	66 mg	
SODIUM	809 mg	

Spicy Grilled Pork

2 tablespoons chili powder
1 teaspoon salt
¼ teaspoon ginger
¼ teaspoon thyme
¼ teaspoon pepper
2 pounds pork tenderloin (2 tenderloins,
    about 1 pound each)

Mix together chili powder, salt, ginger, thyme, and pepper. Rub spices into tenderloins on all sides. Place in a shallow baking dish, cover tightly, and refrigerate for 2 to 4 hours. Grill tenderloins over hot coals for about 15 minutes per side. Do not undercook; meat is done when juices run clear or the internal temperature reaches 160 degrees F. Makes 8 servings.

NUTRITION (PER SERVING): 173 CALORIES

TOTAL FAT	5 g	(26% OF CALORIES)
PROTEIN	29 g	(67% OF CALORIES)
CARBOHYDRATES	1 g	(7% OF CALORIES)
CHOLESTEROL	92 mg	
SODIUM	330 mg	

Veal Mostaccioli

2 cups peeled and cubed eggplants (about 1 pound)
2 cups cubed yellow squash (about 1 pound)
½ pound small whole fresh mushrooms
2 tablespoons balsamic vinegar, divided
2 teaspoons olive oil
1 pound lean ground veal
1 cup chopped onions
¾ teaspoon salt, divided
2 cloves garlic, minced
½ teaspoon red pepper
2 cans (14½ ounces each) chopped
    stewed tomatoes, undrained
6 cups cooked mostaccioli
¼ cup freshly grated Parmesan cheese
¼ cup minced fresh basil

In a 15 x 10-inch jelly-roll pan, arrange eggplants, squash, and mushrooms in a single layer. Drizzle 1 tablespoon vinegar and olive oil over vegetables. Bake at 400 degrees F. for 8 minutes. Turn vegetables over and bake an additional 10 minutes until tender and browned. Set aside.

In a nonstick skillet over medium heat, cook the veal, onions, ¼ teaspoon salt, and garlic until veal is browned, stirring to crumble. Drain and pat dry with paper towels. Return to skillet. Add remaining ½ teaspoon salt, red pepper, and tomatoes with liquid. Stir well. Bring to a boil. Reduce heat and simmer, uncovered, for 10 minutes, stirring occasionally.

Combine eggplant mixture, veal mixture, mostaccioli, and remaining tablespoon vinegar in a large bowl. Toss well. Sprinkle with Parmesan cheese and basil. Makes 6 servings.

NUTRITION (PER SERVING): 279 CALORIES

TOTAL FAT	8 g	(25% OF CALORIES)
PROTEIN	21 g	(30% OF CALORIES)
CARBOHYDRATES	32 g	(45% OF CALORIES)
CHOLESTEROL	76 mg	
SODIUM	499 mg	

Sweet and Sour Pork

2 pounds lean pork, about ½-inch thick
2 tablespoons cornstarch
2 tablespoons soy sauce
2 cups carrots, cut in diagonal chunks
1¼ cups onions (small), cut in quarters
1 clove garlic, minced
1 can (20 ounces) pineapple chunks in juice
½ cup green bell peppers, cut in strips
3 tablespoons cornstarch
2 tablespoons brown sugar
⅔ cup vinegar
½ cup soy sauce
5 cups hot cooked rice

Cut pork into 2-inch strips. Mix 2 tablespoons cornstarch and 2 tablespoons soy sauce; toss with pork strips. Cover and marinate at least 1 hour in refrigerator (can be marinated several hours or overnight). Drain, saving marinade. Spray a large frying pan with nonstick cooking spray; preheat briefly on stove. Add pork and stir-fry until evenly browned and tender (about 10 minutes). Remove meat from pan. Stir-fry carrots, onions, and garlic in same pan. Cover and cook on low heat until tender-crisp, about 10 minutes. Drain pineapple, reserving juice; add to vegetables in pan along with green peppers. Return meat to pan and stir in marinade.

Mix 3 tablespoons cornstarch and the brown sugar in a small saucepan. Measure reserved pineapple juice and add enough water to make 2 cups. Stir this mixture into the cornstarch and sugar, and add vinegar and ½ cup soy sauce. Cook over medium heat, stirring constantly, until thickened and clear. Pour over meat and vegetables; heat until flavors are blended, about 10 minutes. Serve over rice. Makes 10 servings.

NUTRITION (PER SERVING): 382 CALORIES

TOTAL FAT	7 g	(16% OF CALORIES)
PROTEIN	24 g	(25% OF CALORIES)
CARBOHYDRATES	56 g	(58% OF CALORIES)
CHOLESTEROL	57 mg	
SODIUM	1099 mg	

Simple Pork Chop Bake

6 pork chops
6 tablespoons ketchup
6 tablespoons brown sugar
6 slices onion
6 slices lemon

Trim all visible fat from pork chops. Arrange chops in a 13 x 9-inch baking pan. Spread each pork chop with 1 tablespoon ketchup and sprinkle with 1 tablespoon brown sugar. Top each with 1 slice of onion and 1 lemon slice. Bake, uncovered, at 350 degrees F. for 45 minutes to 1 hour, depending on thickness of chops. Makes 6 servings.

NUTRITION (PER SERVING): 199 CALORIES

TOTAL FAT	10 g	(45% OF CALORIES)
PROTEIN	23 g	(46% OF CALORIES)
CARBOHYDRATES	17 g	(9% OF CALORIES)
CHOLESTEROL	94 mg	
SODIUM	257 mg	

Pork Chow Mein

1 pound lean pork, cubed
1 cup chopped onions
1 cup celery, sliced diagonally
½ cup canned sliced bamboo shoots
1 cup sliced fresh mushrooms
1 cup fresh bean sprouts
1 cup chicken broth
2 tablespoons soy sauce
½ teaspoon sugar
1½ tablespoons cornstarch
2 tablespoons water

Spray a large frying pan with nonstick cooking spray. Add pork cubes and stir-fry until browned and tender. Remove meat from pan. Add vegetables and stir-fry for about 5 minutes. (Do not overcook; vegetables should be crisp.) Combine the meat and vegetables; mix well.

Mix chicken broth, soy sauce, and sugar in a small saucepan. Make a paste of cornstarch and water; stir into the hot broth mixture. Cook, stirring constantly, until thickened. Pour over meat and vegetables. Let sit for 10 minutes to blend flavors before serving. Serve over chow mein noodles or rice. Makes 8 servings.

NUTRITION (PER SERVING): 119 CALORIES

TOTAL FAT	4 g	(33% OF CALORIES)
PROTEIN	14 g	(47% OF CALORIES)
CARBOHYDRATES	6 g	(20% OF CALORIES)
CHOLESTEROL	36 mg	
SODIUM	492 mg	

Pork Chops with Scalloped Potatoes

3 tablespoons butter or margarine
3 tablespoons flour
1½ teaspoons salt
¼ teaspoon pepper
1 can (14½ ounces) low-sodium chicken broth
6 pork loin chops (about ¾-inch thick)
2 tablespoons vegetable oil
½ teaspoon sage (optional)
Salt and pepper
6 cups potatoes, peeled and thinly sliced
1 onion, sliced
Paprika
Chopped fresh parsley

Melt butter or margarine in a small saucepan; stir in flour, salt, and pepper. Add chicken broth and cook over medium heat, stirring constantly, until mixture thickens and bubbles. Cook 1 minute longer and remove from heat. Heat oil in a large frying pan; add pork chops and cook until browned. Season with sage if desired, and salt and pepper to taste. Spray a 13 x 9-inch baking dish with nonstick cooking spray. Layer potatoes and onion slices in dish and pour the broth mixture over them. Arrange the pork chops on top of the potatoes. Cover dish tightly with aluminum foil and bake at 350 degrees F. for 1 hour. Uncover and bake an additional 30 minutes or until potatoes are tender. Sprinkle with paprika and parsley. Makes 6 servings.

NUTRITION (PER SERVING): 437 CALORIES

TOTAL FAT	18 g	(37% OF CALORIES)
PROTEIN	27 g	(24% OF CALORIES)
CARBOHYDRATES	43 g	(39% OF CALORIES)
CHOLESTEROL	77 mg	
SODIUM	1140 mg	

Filipino Tacos

¼ cup sugar
1 tablespoon cornstarch
1 cup chicken broth
2 tablespoons light soy sauce
1 clove garlic, minced
1 small onion, chopped
2 cloves garlic, minced
2 tablespoons vegetable oil
8 ounces lean boneless pork, cooked and diced
½ cup cooked shrimp
¼ cup chopped lean cooked ham
½ cup cooked garbanzo beans
2 carrots, cut in julienne strips
½ cup frozen French-style green beans, thawed
¼ cup water
2 cups shredded cabbage
1 teaspoon salt
18 egg-roll skins
Lettuce leaves

Make sauce: In a small saucepan mix together sugar, cornstarch, chicken broth, and soy sauce. Cook over medium heat, stirring constantly, until mixture thickens, about 2 minutes. Stir in 1 clove minced garlic. Makes about 1 cup sauce.

Make filling: In a skillet, cook onion and 2 cloves minced garlic in hot oil till tender. Add pork, shrimp, ham, and garbanzos. Simmer, uncovered, stirring frequently, for 5 minutes. Add carrot strips, thawed green beans, and water. Cook, covered, for 5 minutes. Stir in cabbage and 1 teaspoon salt; cook, covered, 7 minutes or until vegetables are tender. Cool.

Prepare egg-roll skins: Brush a little cooking oil in a large shallow skillet. Preheat briefly on stove. Place an egg-roll skin in skillet and cook on one side only over medium heat for 30 to 45 seconds, until light brown. Turn out onto paper towel. Repeat with remaining skins. Add oil to skillet from time to time if needed.

Assemble rolls: Place an egg-roll skin, unbrowned side up, with one corner facing you. Top with a lettuce leaf and fill with about ⅓ cup of the meat and vegetable mixture. Roll up, folding in one end of egg-roll skin and leaving other end open. Repeat with remaining ingredients. Spoon sauce into open end of rolls and serve immediately. Makes 6 servings, 3 rolls each.

NUTRITION (PER SERVING): 265 CALORIES

TOTAL FAT	9 g	(30% OF CALORIES)
PROTEIN	17 g	(26% OF CALORIES)
CARBOHYDRATES	29 g	(44% OF CALORIES)
CHOLESTEROL	60 mg	
SODIUM	814 mg	

Piquant Pork Chops

8 thin-cut pork loin chops
1 teaspoon cumin
½ teaspoon ginger
½ teaspoon coriander
¼ teaspoon turmeric
⅛ teaspoon salt
2 bay leaves, well crumbled

Trim all visible fat from pork chops. Mix together the cumin, ginger, coriander, turmeric, salt, and crumbled bay leaves. Rub mixture into pork chops, coating both sides of each chop. Arrange chops in a 13 x 9-inch glass baking dish, cover, and let stand for 1 hour at room temperature. Preheat broiler (chops may also be cooked on a barbecue grill). Place pork chops on broiler rack and broil 7 to 8 inches from heat, turning occasionally, until cooked through (about 8 to 10 minutes). Makes 4 servings, 2 pork chops each.

NUTRITION (PER SERVING): 315 CALORIES

TOTAL FAT	14 g	(41% OF CALORIES)
PROTEIN	44 g	(55% OF CALORIES)
CARBOHYDRATES	3 g	(4% OF CALORIES)
CHOLESTEROL	123 mg	
SODIUM	204 mg	

Easy Pork Chops Dijon

6 pork loin chops
½ cup wine vinegar
¼ cup Dijon-style mustard
2 tablespoons finely chopped green onions
2 teaspoons tarragon
¼ teaspoon coarsely ground black pepper

Trim all visible fat from pork chops. Mix together the vinegar, mustard, green onions, tarragon, and pepper. Spray a 13 x 9-inch baking dish with nonstick cooking spray. Arrange pork chops in dish and spoon 1 tablespoon of mustard mixture over each chop. Bake at 425 degrees F. for 10 minutes. Turn chops over and spread with remaining marinade. Return dish to oven and bake 8 to 10 minutes more, or until cooked through. Makes 6 servings.

NUTRITION (PER SERVING): 167 CALORIES

TOTAL FAT	8 g	(41% OF CALORIES)
PROTEIN	22 g	(54% OF CALORIES)
CARBOHYDRATES	2 g	(5% OF CALORIES)
CHOLESTEROL	62 mg	
SODIUM	317 mg	

One-Dish Pork Chop Dinner

4 pork loin chops
¼ teaspoon sage (optional)
¼ teaspoon rosemary (optional)
4 potatoes, peeled and sliced
4 carrots, cut in ½-inch diagonal slices
2 onions, sliced
½ teaspoon salt
¼ teaspoon pepper
1 can (14 ounces) chicken broth

Preheat oven to 375 degrees F. Trim all visible fat from pork chops. Rub chops with sage and rosemary, if desired. Brown chops in a large nonstick frying pan over medium heat. Spray a 9-inch square baking dish with nonstick cooking spray. Arrange browned pork chops in the dish and cover with a layer of potatoes, a layer of carrots, and a layer of onions. Sprinkle with salt and pepper and pour broth over the top. Cover with aluminum foil and bake for 1 hour, or until chops are tender. Makes 4 servings.

NUTRITION (PER SERVING): 356 CALORIES

TOTAL FAT	9 g	(24% OF CALORIES)
PROTEIN	27 g	(31% OF CALORIES)
CARBOHYDRATES	39 g	(45% OF CALORIES)
CHOLESTEROL	72 mg	
SODIUM	614 mg	

Cranberry-Glazed Pork Roast

1 can (16 ounces) jellied cranberry sauce
½ cup sugar
½ cup cranberry juice cocktail
1 teaspoon dry mustard
¼ teaspoon cloves
1 boneless extra-lean sirloin pork roast (3 pounds)
2 tablespoons cornstarch
2 tablespoons cold water
Salt to taste

In a medium bowl, mash cranberry sauce with a fork or a potato masher. Stir in sugar, cranberry juice, mustard, and cloves. Place pork roast in slow cooker and pour cranberry sauce mixture over it. Cook on low setting for 6 to 8 hours or until meat is tender. Remove roast and keep warm. With a metal spoon, skim the fat from the liquid in the slow cooker. Pour 2 cups of the liquid (add water to fill out the measure, if necessary) into a small saucepan. Bring to a boil over medium-high heat. Blend the cornstarch and cold water to make a paste; stir gradually into boiling liquid. Continue cooking, stirring constantly, until mixture thickens. Add salt to taste. Serve with pork. Makes 12 servings.

NUTRITION (PER SERVING): 316 CALORIES

TOTAL FAT	10 g	(29% OF CALORIES)
PROTEIN	30 g	(38% OF CALORIES)
CARBOHYDRATES	26 g	(33% OF CALORIES)
CHOLESTEROL	92 mg	
SODIUM	64 mg	

Grilled Ham with Pineapple Sauce

1 small can (8 ounces) crushed pineapple, drained
2 tablespoons orange marmalade
1 tablespoon chopped fresh cilantro or parsley
2 teaspoons chopped jalapeños, fresh or canned
2 teaspoons lime juice
¼ teaspoon salt
1½ pounds cooked extra-lean ham,
*   sliced ¾- to 1-inch thick*

In a small bowl, combine pineapple, marmalade, cilantro or parsley, jalapeños, lime juice, and salt. Mix well and chill in refrigerator to blend flavors. Grill ham 4 to 6 inches from coals for 10 to 20 minutes, turning 2 or 3 times, until heated thoroughly. Serve with pineapple sauce. Makes 6 servings.

NUTRITION (PER SERVING): 183 CALORIES

TOTAL FAT	6 g	(29% OF CALORIES)
PROTEIN	22 g	(48% OF CALORIES)
CARBOHYDRATES	11 g	(23% OF CALORIES)
CHOLESTEROL	53 mg	
SODIUM	1721 mg	

Lemony Lamb Chops

4 lamb chops, ¾-inch thick
2 teaspoons cornstarch
¼ teaspoon salt
⅛ teaspoon oregano
1 dash pepper
½ cup water
1 teaspoon Worcestershire sauce
¼ teaspoon finely shredded lemon peel
2 tablespoons lemon juice

Trim all visible fat from lamb chops and place them on rack of broiler pan. Set aside. In a small saucepan, mix together cornstarch, salt, oregano, and pepper. Stir in water and Worcestershire sauce. Cook over medium heat, stirring constantly, until mixture thickens and bubbles; continue cooking and stirring for an additional 2 minutes. Add lemon peel and juice. Brush sauce on lamb chops. Broil chops 3 to 4 inches from heat for 10 to 16 minutes (depending on desired degree of doneness). Turn chops halfway through broiling time and brush again with sauce. Serve lamb chops with remaining sauce. Makes 4 servings.

NUTRITION (PER SERVING): 229 CALORIES

TOTAL FAT	10 g	(41% OF CALORIES)
PROTEIN	32 g	(56% OF CALORIES)
CARBOHYDRATES	2 g	(4% OF CALORIES)
CHOLESTEROL	101 mg	
SODIUM	239 mg	

CHICKEN AND TURKEY

Baked Chicken Breasts Supreme

1½ cups nonfat plain yogurt or nonfat sour cream
¼ cup lemon juice
½ teaspoon Worcestershire sauce
½ teaspoon celery seed
½ teaspoon Hungarian sweet paprika
1 clove garlic, minced
½ teaspoon salt
¼ teaspoon pepper
2 pounds skinless boneless chicken breast halves
2 cups dry bread crumbs

Mix together yogurt or sour cream, lemon juice, Worcestershire sauce, celery seed, paprika, garlic, salt, and pepper. Wash chicken breasts and pat dry with paper towel. Dip each piece in yogurt mixture to coat thoroughly. Place chicken pieces in large bowl and pour yogurt over; cover tightly and refrigerate overnight.

When ready to bake, preheat oven to 350 degrees F. Remove chicken pieces from yogurt mixture and dredge in bread crumbs. Place in a 13 x 9-inch baking dish. Bake, uncovered, for 45 minutes to 1 hour, or until chicken is fork tender and juices run clear. Makes 8 servings.

NUTRITION (PER SERVING): 242 CALORIES

TOTAL FAT	3 g	(10% OF CALORIES)
PROTEIN	32 g	(53% OF CALORIES)
CARBOHYDRATES	23 g	(37% OF CALORIES)
CHOLESTEROL	68 mg	
SODIUM	438 mg	

Basil Chicken with Rice

1 tablespoon olive oil
1 clove garlic, minced
1 pound skinless boneless chicken breasts, cut into bite-size chunks
1 zucchini, cut into chunks
¼ pound small fresh mushrooms, halved
2 tomatoes, cut into chunks
1 tablespoon vinegar
1 tablespoon basil
¼ teaspoon pepper
3 cups hot cooked rice

In a large frying pan, sauté garlic 1 to 2 minutes in heated oil. Add chicken and stir-fry over medium heat until no longer pink. While chicken is cooking, gently toss together the zucchini, mushrooms, tomatoes, vinegar, basil, and pepper until vegetables are well coated. Remove chicken from pan and set aside. Stir-fry vegetables for 5 to 7 minutes, until tender-crisp. Add chicken to skillet and stir over heat until heated through. Serve over rice. Makes 4 servings.

NUTRITION (PER SERVING): 260 CALORIES

TOTAL FAT	5 g	(16% OF CALORIES)
PROTEIN	18 g	(28% OF CALORIES)
CARBOHYDRATES	36 g	(56% OF CALORIES)
CHOLESTEROL	34 mg	
SODIUM	47 mg	

Chicken Curry Salad with Fruit

1½ pounds skinless boneless chicken breasts,
    cooked and diced
1 cup diced celery
⅔ cup nonfat mayonnaise
2 tablespoons lemon juice
½ teaspoon salt
1 teaspoon curry powder
3 tablespoons blanched slivered almonds
½ cantaloupe, cut into wedges
1 cup seedless grapes
1 cup canned pineapple chunks, drained

Mix chicken and celery together in a medium bowl.
Blend mayonnaise, lemon juice, salt, and curry
powder. Pour over the chicken mixture and toss
lightly. Cover and chill in refrigerator. Just before
serving, mound salad in center of a serving platter
lined with salad greens. Sprinkle with slivered
almonds. Garnish with fruits. Makes 6 servings.

NUTRITION (PER SERVING): 241 CALORIES

TOTAL FAT	5 g	(19% OF CALORIES)
PROTEIN	28 g	(46% OF CALORIES)
CARBOHYDRATES	21 g	(35% OF CALORIES)
CHOLESTEROL	66 mg	
SODIUM	618 mg	

Garden Chicken Salad

Pictured on page 45.

2 tablespoons vegetable oil
2 tablespoons lemon juice
2 tablespoons toasted sesame seeds
1½ teaspoons soy sauce
½ teaspoon salt
¼ teaspoon pepper
¼ teaspoon dry mustard
2 pounds skinless boneless chicken breasts,
    cooked and shredded
2 cups shredded lettuce
1 cup carrots, cut in julienne strips
1 cup cucumbers, cut in julienne strips
⅔ cup green onions, cut in 2-inch strips
1 cup fresh bean sprouts

Blend the oil, lemon juice, sesame seeds, soy sauce,
salt, pepper, and mustard in a small bowl. Cover
and refrigerate to blend flavors. In a large salad
bowl, combine the chicken, lettuce, carrots,
cucumbers, green onions, and bean sprouts. Cover
and refrigerate until ready to serve. Just before
serving, pour dressing over salad and toss gently.
Makes 10 servings.

NUTRITION (PER SERVING): 149 CALORIES

TOTAL FAT	5 g	(30% OF CALORIES)
PROTEIN	22 g	(59% OF CALORIES)
CARBOHYDRATES	4 g	(11% OF CALORIES)
CHOLESTEROL	53 mg	
SODIUM	222 mg	

Tropical Chicken Salad

1½ tablespoons lime juice

1½ tablespoons honey

⅔ cup nonfat mayonnaise

1 container (4 ounces) low-fat peach yogurt

½ teaspoon lemon pepper

2 pounds skinless boneless chicken breasts,
   cooked and diced

1 pound seedless green or red grapes

1 can (15 ounces) pineapple tidbits in juice, drained

¼ cup chopped celery

⅓ cup diced green bell peppers

Lettuce leaves

1 can (11 ounces) mandarin oranges, drained

½ cup sliced almonds, toasted

Mix lime juice and honey together in a small bowl. Add mayonnaise, yogurt, and lemon pepper; mix well and set in refrigerator to blend flavors. In a large bowl combine chicken, grapes, pineapple, celery, and green peppers. Refrigerate. Just before serving, pour dressing over salad and toss gently to mix. Place a lettuce leaf on a salad plate, spoon salad on top of lettuce, and garnish with mandarin oranges and sliced almonds. Serve immediately. Makes 8 servings.

NUTRITION (PER SERVING): 303 CALORIES

TOTAL FAT	7 g	(21% OF CALORIES)
PROTEIN	30 g	(39% OF CALORIES)
CARBOHYDRATES	30 g	(40% OF CALORIES)
CHOLESTEROL	66 mg	
SODIUM	368 mg	

Hot Chicken Salad

2 tablespoons lemon juice

1 cup nonfat mayonnaise

¼ cup light sour cream

12 ounces skinless boneless chicken breasts,
   cooked and cut in chunks

2½ cups chopped celery

½ cup chopped onions

1 cup shredded fat-free cheddar cheese

½ teaspoon seasoned salt

¾ cup crushed reduced-sodium pretzels

Combine lemon juice, mayonnaise, and sour cream in a large bowl. Add chicken, celery, onions, cheese, and seasoned salt and mix well. Spray a 1½ quart casserole dish with nonstick cooking spray; pour salad mixture in. Sprinkle crushed pretzels on top and bake at 375 degrees F. for 25 minutes. Serve immediately. Makes 8 servings.

NUTRITION (PER SERVING): 169 CALORIES

TOTAL FAT	6 g	(32% OF CALORIES)
PROTEIN	15 g	(35% OF CALORIES)
CARBOHYDRATES	14 g	(33% OF CALORIES)
CHOLESTEROL	41 mg	
SODIUM	869 mg	

Tarragon Chicken

1 pound skinless boneless chicken breast halves
2 tablespoons thinly sliced green onions
½ teaspoon tarragon
Salt and pepper
1 tablespoon butter or margarine
½ cup chicken broth
1 tablespoon grated Parmesan cheese
1 tablespoon chopped fresh parsley

Preheat oven to 350 degrees F. Place chicken in a 13 x 9-inch glass baking dish; sprinkle with green onions, tarragon, salt, and pepper. Dot with butter or margarine. Add broth to dish. Bake, uncovered, for 45 minutes. Sprinkle with Parmesan cheese and bake an additional five minutes to brown lightly. Just before serving, sprinkle with chopped parsley. Makes 4 servings.

NUTRITION (PER SERVING): 165 CALORIES

TOTAL FAT	5 g	(27% OF CALORIES)
PROTEIN	29 g	(71% OF CALORIES)
CARBOHYDRATES	1 g	(2% OF CALORIES)
CHOLESTEROL	75 mg	
SODIUM	327 mg	

Baked Cajun Chicken and Vegetables

2 onions, sliced
1 pound skinless boneless chicken breast tenders
4 cups sliced yellow squash
1 cup sliced fresh mushrooms
8 cherry tomatoes, halved
½ teaspoon Cajun seasoning
1 clove garlic, minced
4 teaspoons butter or margarine

Spray a 10-inch square baking pan with nonstick cooking spray. Arrange sliced onions evenly in pan; top with chicken breast tenders, squash, mushrooms, and tomatoes. Sprinkle evenly with Cajun seasoning and garlic; dot with butter or margarine. Cover pan with aluminum foil. Bake at 325 degrees F. for 60 minutes. Makes 4 servings.

NUTRITION (PER SERVING): 228 CALORIES

TOTAL FAT	6 g	(23% OF CALORIES)
PROTEIN	29 g	(51% OF CALORIES)
CARBOHYDRATES	15 g	(26% OF CALORIES)
CHOLESTEROL	66 mg	
SODIUM	125 mg	

Cheese-Stuffed Chicken Kiev

1 pound skinless boneless chicken breast halves
¼ teaspoon pepper
2 cloves garlic, minced
2 tablespoons minced fresh or
*   freeze-dried chives, divided*
2 ounces part-skim mozzarella cheese,
*   cut into 4 inch-long fingers*
1 egg white
1 tablespoon skim milk
1 tablespoon water
¼ cup flour
⅓ cup dry bread crumbs

Pound the chicken breasts to ¼-inch thickness and sprinkle them with pepper, garlic, and 1 tablespoon of the chives. Wrap a cheese finger in each chicken breast, making a roll and tucking the ends in as you roll. Whisk together the egg white, milk, and water. Pour into a shallow dish. Spread flour on one plate and bread crumbs on another. Coat each chicken roll with flour, then dip in egg mixture and roll in crumbs. Place rolls on a baking rack on a plate or shallow pan and refrigerate, uncovered, for 30 minutes. Preheat oven to 375 degrees F. Arrange rolls in a 9-inch square baking dish and bake, uncovered, 40 to 45 minutes or until golden brown. Sprinkle with the remaining chives. Makes 4 servings.

NUTRITION (PER SERVING): 192 CALORIES

TOTAL FAT	6 g	(30% OF CALORIES)
PROTEIN	20 g	(42% OF CALORIES)
CARBOHYDRATES	13 g	(28% OF CALORIES)
CHOLESTEROL	43 mg	
SODIUM	184 mg	

Dijon Chicken

1 pound skinless boneless chicken breast halves
2 tablespoons Dijon-style mustard
1 teaspoon lemon juice
¼ teaspoon pepper
2 green onions, chopped fine
½ cup soft white bread crumbs

Lightly spray broiler pan with nonstick cooking spray. Preheat broiler for 5 minutes. Arrange chicken pieces on broiler pan and broil 7 to 8 inches from heat for 5 minutes on each side. While chicken is cooking, mix together in a small bowl the mustard, lemon juice, pepper, and green onions. Spread the mixture on both sides of the broiled chicken breasts and return them to broiler pan. Sprinkle with half the bread crumbs. Broil until crumbs are brown, about 2 minutes. Turn chicken pieces and coat other side with remaining bread crumbs. Broil an additional 2 minutes or until no pink shows in the middle of cut chicken breast and juices run clear. Makes 4 servings.

NUTRITION (PER SERVING): 179 CALORIES

TOTAL FAT	3 g	(13% OF CALORIES)
PROTEIN	29 g	(65% OF CALORIES)
CARBOHYDRATES	10 g	(22% OF CALORIES)
CHOLESTEROL	69 mg	
SODIUM	358 mg	

Chicken Alabam

⅓ cup flour
½ teaspoon paprika
½ teaspoon salt
1 dash pepper
1 dash thyme
2 pounds skinless boneless chicken breast halves
3 tablespoons light butter, melted
¼ cup chopped onions
2 tablespoons light butter
1 cup water
1½ teaspoons chicken bouillon granules
½ cup skim milk
¼ teaspoon lemon juice
2 tablespoons chopped pimiento

Preheat oven to 350 degrees F. Mix together flour, paprika, salt, pepper, and thyme. Dredge chicken pieces in flour mixture and arrange in single layer in glass casserole dish. Brush with 3 tablespoons melted light butter. Bake uncovered for 25 minutes. Remove from oven and reduce oven temperature to 225 degrees F.

In a small saucepan, sauté onions in 2 tablespoons light butter until translucent. Stir in excess flour from dredging chicken. Add water and bouillon; cook and stir until thickened. Add skim milk and cook until smooth and thick. Add lemon juice, then pimiento; blend well. Pour sauce over oven-browned chicken; cover and bake at 225 degrees F. an additional 20 to 30 minutes, or until chicken is fork tender. Makes 8 servings.

NUTRITION (PER SERVING): 179 CALORIES

TOTAL FAT	5 g	(27% OF CALORIES)
PROTEIN	27 g	(61% OF CALORIES)
CARBOHYDRATES	5 g	(12% OF CALORIES)
CHOLESTEROL	75 mg	
SODIUM	318 mg	

Chicken Creole

1 pound skinless boneless chicken breast halves
1 teaspoon paprika
¼ teaspoon cayenne pepper
2 tablespoons light butter, divided
¾ cup chopped onions
½ cup chopped green bell peppers
¼ cup chopped celery
2 cloves garlic, minced
1 can (14½ ounces) chopped stewed
    tomatoes, undrained
1 teaspoon rosemary
½ teaspoon marjoram
1 bay leaf
1 tablespoon flour
¼ cup water
3 cups hot cooked rice

Sprinkle the chicken with paprika and cayenne pepper and set aside. In a large frying pan, sauté the onions, bell peppers, celery, and garlic in 1 tablespoon of the butter for 5 minutes over medium heat. Remove vegetables from pan. Turn heat to medium high and melt remaining 1 tablespoon butter in frying pan. Add chicken and cook for about 5 minutes, turning to brown on both sides. Add tomatoes with liquid, rosemary, marjoram, bay leaf, and half of the cooked vegetables. Reduce heat, cover, and simmer for 20 to 25 minutes or until chicken is tender. Blend flour and water until smooth. Stir gradually into frying pan. Cook, stirring constantly, until mixture thickens. Add remaining vegetables and heat through. Remove and discard bay leaf. Serve with rice. Makes 4 servings.

NUTRITION (PER SERVING): 361 CALORIES

TOTAL FAT	5 g	(12% OF CALORIES)
PROTEIN	29 g	(32% OF CALORIES)
CARBOHYDRATES	50 g	(56% OF CALORIES)
CHOLESTEROL	66 mg	
SODIUM	534 mg	

Chicken Tetrazzini

8 ounces dry spaghetti noodles

½ cup diced celery

⅓ cup chopped onions

1 can (8 ounces) mushroom stems
  and pieces, drained

3 cups chopped cooked chicken

1 teaspoon dried parsley flakes

½ teaspoon salt

2 tablespoons light margarine

3½ tablespoons flour

1½ cups chicken broth

1 cup skim milk

¼ teaspoon pepper

2 tablespoons dried parsley flakes

2 tablespoons grated Parmesan cheese

Cook spaghetti according to package directions. Rinse under hot running water; drain thoroughly and set aside.

Spray a large frying pan with nonstick cooking spray; preheat briefly over medium heat. Stir-fry celery, onions, and mushrooms in hot pan until tender, about 5 minutes. Remove from heat and stir in chicken, 1 teaspoon parsley flakes, and salt.

In a small saucepan over low heat, melt margarine. Stir in flour to make a smooth paste; cook 1 minute, stirring constantly. Add chicken broth, milk, and pepper; raise heat to medium and cook, stirring constantly until mixture thickens and bubbles.

In a large bowl, stir together the chicken mixture, spaghetti noodles, and white sauce.

Pour into a 3-quart casserole; sprinkle with 2 tablespoons parsley flakes and Parmesan cheese. Bake 20 to 25 minutes at 350 degrees F. Makes 10 servings.

NUTRITION (PER SERVING): 204 CALORIES

TOTAL FAT	4 g	(18% OF CALORIES)
PROTEIN	20 g	(39% OF CALORIES)
CARBOHYDRATES	22 g	(43% OF CALORIES)
CHOLESTEROL	37 mg	
SODIUM	462 mg	

Chicken Cordon Bleu

Pictured on page 63.

4 skinless boneless chicken breast halves

¼ teaspoon pepper

4 slices (1 ounce each) extra-lean boneless ham

¾ cup shredded part-skim mozzarella cheese

½ teaspoon paprika

¼ teaspoon garlic powder

½ cup cornflake crumbs

⅓ cup skim milk

Place each chicken breast half between sheets of plastic wrap and pound to about ¼-inch thickness. Sprinkle with pepper and top with a piece of ham and 3 tablespoons cheese. Roll up like a jelly roll. Tuck in ends and secure with wooden toothpicks. Spray an 11 x 7-inch baking dish with cooking spray and set aside. In a shallow dish, combine paprika, garlic powder, and cornflake crumbs. Dip each chicken roll in milk, then roll in cornflake crumb mixture, turning to coat thoroughly. Place rolls in the prepared baking dish. Bake, uncovered, at 350 degrees F. for 30 minutes or until chicken is fork tender. Makes 4 servings.

NUTRITION (PER SERVING): 204 CALORIES

TOTAL FAT	6 g	(26% OF CALORIES)
PROTEIN	36 g	(70% OF CALORIES)
CARBOHYDRATES	2 g	(4% OF CALORIES)
CHOLESTEROL	87 mg	
SODIUM	268 mg	

Chicken Fajitas

1½ pounds skinless boneless chicken breasts
1 cup water
1 package fajita seasoning mix
2 tablespoons olive oil
2 onions, sliced
1 green bell pepper, sliced in strips
1 red bell pepper, sliced in strips
12 nonfat flour tortillas
¼ cup nonfat sour cream
½ cup salsa

Cut chicken breasts into strips. Stir together 1 cup water and the fajita seasoning mix; add chicken strips and marinate in refrigerator for 2 hours. Heat oil in heavy saucepan and sauté onions and green and red peppers until tender-crisp. Remove vegetables from pan and add chicken strips, reserving marinade. Sauté chicken until light brown. Add leftover marinade and simmer for 5 minutes. Return vegetables to pan and heat to mingle flavors. Spoon mixture onto warm tortillas. Fold over and garnish with nonfat sour cream and salsa. Makes 6 servings.

NUTRITION (PER SERVING): 273 CALORIES

TOTAL FAT	9 g	(30% OF CALORIES)
PROTEIN	29 g	(42% OF CALORIES)
CARBOHYDRATES	19 g	(28% OF CALORIES)
CHOLESTEROL	70 mg	
SODIUM	574 mg	

Chicken Enchiladas

¾ pound skinless boneless chicken breasts,
    cut in strips
2 cups chopped white onions
¼ cup light sour cream
¼ cup nonfat mayonnaise
1 can (14 ounces) chicken broth (chill broth
    beforehand and skim fat off top)
1½ cups shredded reduced-fat
    cheddar cheese, divided
8 6-inch corn tortillas
1 can (8 ounces) enchilada sauce

Brown chicken strips over medium heat in skillet sprayed with nonstick cooking spray. When the chicken is golden brown, add onions and cook for 5 to 7 minutes more or until onions are tender. Remove from heat and set aside. In a small saucepan, combine sour cream and mayonnaise. Very gradually add chicken broth to sour cream mixture, stirring constantly. Do not add broth too fast or mixture will be lumpy. When thoroughly mixed, place saucepan over medium heat. Cook, stirring constantly, until mixture starts to boil. Add 1 cup of the shredded cheese and stir over heat until cheese is melted. Set aside.

Spray a 9-inch square baking dish with nonstick cooking spray; set aside. Pour enchilada sauce into a large shallow bowl. Dip 1 corn tortilla in the enchilada sauce, making sure both sides are covered with sauce. Remove tortilla from sauce and fill with slices of chicken meat, browned onion, and a little cheese. (Save some cheese for topping.) Roll tortilla around filling and place in prepared baking dish. Repeat with remaining tortillas. Pour sour cream mixture over filled tortillas. Sprinkle top with remaining cheese. Cover dish with aluminum foil and bake at 375 degrees F. for 20 to 25 minutes. Makes 8 servings.

NUTRITION (PER SERVING): 232 CALORIES

TOTAL FAT	7 g	(27% OF CALORIES)
PROTEIN	21 g	(37% OF CALORIES)
CARBOHYDRATES	21 g	(36% OF CALORIES)
CHOLESTEROL	37 mg	
SODIUM	421 mg	

Quick Fruit Salad (page 103), Chicken Cordon Bleu (page 61), Quick and Easy Carrots (page 113), Wild Rice Pilaf (page 95)

Barbecued Chicken Thighs

1 teaspoon olive oil
¾ cup chopped onions
2 cloves garlic, minced
1 can (14½ ounces) chopped stewed
    tomatoes, undrained
2 tablespoons cider vinegar
2 tablespoons dark molasses
1 tablespoon prepared mustard
1 teaspoon salt
½ teaspoon chili powder
⅛ teaspoon cayenne pepper
8 skinless chicken thighs

Heat olive oil in a heavy 2-quart saucepan over medium heat. Sauté onions and garlic in hot oil until soft, about 5 minutes. Stir in tomatoes with liquid, vinegar, molasses, mustard, salt, chili powder, and cayenne pepper. Heat to simmering point; reduce heat and simmer, uncovered, about 20 minutes. Cool to room temperature. Pour into container of electric blender or food processor and puree for 30 seconds. Reserve 1 cup of sauce to be used later.

Place chicken thighs in a shallow baking dish. Pour the remaining sauce over the chicken, turning to coat on all sides. Cover and let stand in refrigerator at least 4 hours, turning the chicken pieces occasionally.

Spray the rack of a broiler pan lightly with nonstick cooking spray. Preheat the broiler for 5 minutes. Remove chicken from marinade and place on rack. Broil chicken 7 to 9 inches from the heat for 15 minutes, basting occasionally with the reserved 1 cup sauce. Turn pieces over and broil an additional 15 minutes or until browned, basting occasionally. Serve any remaining sauce with chicken, if desired. Makes 4 servings.

NUTRITION (PER SERVING): 288 CALORIES

TOTAL FAT	13 g	(40% OF CALORIES)
PROTEIN	29 g	(40% OF CALORIES)
CARBOHYDRATES	14 g	(20% OF CALORIES)
CHOLESTEROL	98 mg	
SODIUM	754 mg	

Stuffed Chicken Breasts

½ cup uncooked brown rice
1 cup low-sodium chicken broth
1 pound skinless boneless chicken breast halves
½ teaspoon pepper, divided
¼ teaspoon salt
¼ cup finely chopped tomatoes
¼ cup finely shredded part-skim mozzarella cheese
1 teaspoon basil

Cook rice according to package directions, substituting chicken broth for water. Pound chicken breasts to ¼-inch thickness. Sprinkle with ¼ teaspoon pepper and salt. Combine cooked rice, tomatoes, cheese, basil, and remaining ¼ teaspoon pepper. Spoon rice mixture on top of chicken breasts; fold over and secure sides with wooden toothpicks. Wipe off outsides of chicken breasts with paper towel.

Spray a large frying pan with nonstick cooking spray. Add stuffed chicken breasts and cook over medium-high heat 1 minute on each side or just until golden brown. Transfer chicken to shallow baking pan. Bake at 350 degrees F. for 8 to 10 minutes. Makes 4 servings.

NUTRITION (PER SERVING): 209 CALORIES

TOTAL FAT	3 g	(15% OF CALORIES)
PROTEIN	31 g	(59% OF CALORIES)
CARBOHYDRATES	14 g	(27% OF CALORIES)
CHOLESTEROL	70 mg	
SODIUM	291 mg	

Lion House Chicken Crepes

2 egg whites

1 whole egg

½ cup skim milk

½ cup water

3 tablespoons light butter, melted

¾ cup flour

½ teaspoon salt

3 cups chicken broth

¼ cup cornstarch

½ cup water

1 ½ pounds skinless boneless chicken breasts,
    cooked and diced

¼ cup grated cheddar cheese

Make crepes: Combine egg whites, egg, milk, ½ cup water, light butter, flour, and salt in blender container. Blend about 1 minute, scrape down sides with rubber spatula, and blend an additional 30 seconds. Refrigerate for 1 hour. Heat frying pan over medium heat until a drop of water sizzles when dropped on surface. Brush lightly with melted light butter. Pour in just enough batter to cover bottom of pan, tipping and tilting pan to spread batter quickly over bottom. If crepe has holes, add a drop or two of batter to patch. Cook until light brown on bottom and dry on top. Remove from pan and stack on plate. Repeat with remaining batter; recipe makes 12 crepes.

Make chicken glaze: Heat chicken broth in a medium saucepan over medium-high heat. While broth is heating, mix cornstarch with cold water until smooth. Stir gradually into broth, cooking and stirring until thickened. Mix about ½ cup chicken glaze with chicken pieces to moisten.

Assemble crepes: Arrange chicken pieces in center of each crepe. Sprinkle with grated cheese. Fold over sides and place in a 13 x 9-inch baking pan. Bake at 350-degree F. for 15 minutes or until heated through. To serve, place 2 crepes per serving on plate and spoon leftover chicken glaze over top. Makes 6 servings.

NUTRITION (PER SERVING): 305 CALORIES

TOTAL FAT	9 g	(27% OF CALORIES)
PROTEIN	37 g	(48% OF CALORIES)
CARBOHYDRATES	19 g	(25% OF CALORIES)
CHOLESTEROL	108 mg	
SODIUM	1177 mg	

Chicken Kabobs

1 small bottle (8 ounces) oil-free Italian dressing
¼ cup light soy sauce
¼ cup Worcestershire sauce
2 tablespoons lemon juice
1 teaspoon Dijon-style mustard
1½ pounds skinless boneless chicken breast halves
2 green bell peppers, cut into 1½-inch pieces
2 large onions, cut into wedges
18 whole fresh mushrooms

Mix together the Italian dressing, soy sauce, Worcestershire sauce, lemon juice, and mustard. Cut the chicken lengthwise into about 18 strips. Place in a large bowl along with peppers, onions, and mushrooms. Pour marinade over and mix well. Cover and place in refrigerator at least 4 hours (or overnight, if desired), stirring occasionally. Drain marinade and reserve it. Thread chicken alternately with vegetables on skewers. (If using wooden skewers, soak them in water for 30 minutes prior to cooking, to prevent burning.) Grill over medium-hot coals until chicken is no longer pink and juices run clear, about 13 to 15 minutes. Skewers may also be placed under broiler, 6 to 8 inches from heat. Turn occasionally and baste with marinade during cooking time for either method. Makes 6 servings.

NUTRITION (PER SERVING): 229 CALORIES

TOTAL FAT	2 g	(7% OF CALORIES)
PROTEIN	30 g	(52% OF CALORIES)
CARBOHYDRATES	24 g	(41% OF CALORIES)
CHOLESTEROL	66 mg	
SODIUM	673 mg	

Sweet and Hickory Smoke Chicken

1 large onion, sliced thin
6 chicken breast halves, skin removed
½ teaspoon hickory-smoked salt
¼ teaspoon pepper
½ cup ketchup
¼ cup real maple syrup
1 to 2 tablespoons prepared mustard

Arrange onion slices in a layer in the bottom of a 13 x 9-inch baking dish. Place chicken breasts in a single layer on top of onions. Sprinkle with hickory-smoked salt and pepper. In a small bowl, combine ketchup, syrup, and mustard; pour over the chicken. Bake, uncovered, at 350 degrees F. for 1 hour or until chicken is fork tender. Makes 6 servings.

NUTRITION (PER SERVING): 195 CALORIES

TOTAL FAT	3 g	(14% OF CALORIES)
PROTEIN	27 g	(55% OF CALORIES)
CARBOHYDRATES	15 g	(31% OF CALORIES)
CHOLESTEROL	96 mg	
SODIUM	683 mg	

Grilled Lemon Chicken

1 pound skinless boneless chicken breast halves
2 tablespoons honey
1 tablespoon lemon juice
1 tablespoon light soy sauce
1 teaspoon grated lemon peel
½ cup water
1 tablespoon lemon juice
1 tablespoon honey
1 tablespoon cornstarch
1 teaspoon grated lemon peel
½ teaspoon chicken bouillon granules

Arrange chicken breast halves in an 8-inch square glass baking dish. In a small bowl, combine 2 tablespoons honey, 1 tablespoon lemon juice, soy sauce, and 1 teaspoon lemon peel. Pour over chicken, cover, and marinate in refrigerator for 2 to 3 hours. Remove chicken and discard liquid. Grill on hot grill or under broiler until juices run clear and chicken is no longer pink. While chicken is cooking, combine water, 1 tablespoon lemon juice, 1 tablespoon honey, cornstarch, 1 teaspoon lemon peel, and bouillon granules in a small microwave-safe bowl. Microwave on high for 3 to 4 minutes, stirring after every minute, until sauce is thickened and clear. (Sauce may also be made on stove; combine ingredients in small saucepan and cook, stirring constantly, over medium heat until thickened.) Serve over grilled chicken. Makes 4 servings.

NUTRITION (PER SERVING): 190 CALORIES

TOTAL FAT	2 g	(9% OF CALORIES)
PROTEIN	27 g	(57% OF CALORIES)
CARBOHYDRATES	16 g	(34% OF CALORIES)
CHOLESTEROL	68 mg	
SODIUM	204 mg	

Polynesian Chicken

1½ pounds skinless boneless chicken breast halves
1 can (20 ounces) pineapple chunks in juice
¾ cup cider vinegar
½ cup honey
2 tablespoons cornstarch
1 tablespoon soy sauce
¼ teaspoon ginger
1 chicken bouillon cube
½ cup green bell peppers, cut into ¼-inch strips

Arrange chicken pieces in a single layer in a 2-quart baking dish. Bake uncovered at 400 degrees F. for 20 minutes, turning several times. Remove from oven and reduce heat to 350 degrees F.

Drain pineapple, reserving juice. Pour juice into measuring cup and add water to make 1½ cups. Pour into a small saucepan and stir in vinegar, honey, cornstarch, soy sauce, ginger, and bouillon cube; bring to a boil and boil 2 minutes, stirring constantly. Pour over chicken pieces in baking dish. Bake, covered, at 350 degrees F. for 30 minutes. Add pineapple chunks and green pepper. Bake uncovered for 30 minutes longer or until chicken is tender. Serve with cooked rice. Makes 8 servings.

NUTRITION (PER SERVING): 226 CALORIES

TOTAL FAT	2 g	(8% OF CALORIES)
PROTEIN	20 g	(35% OF CALORIES)
CARBOHYDRATES	32 g	(57% OF CALORIES)
CHOLESTEROL	49 mg	
SODIUM	308 mg	

Garlic Chicken and Mushrooms

¼ cup flour
¼ teaspoon pepper
1 pound skinless boneless chicken breast halves
1 tablespoon olive oil
6 cloves garlic, peeled and left whole
¾ pound small fresh mushrooms, halved
¼ cup balsamic vinegar
¾ cup low-sodium chicken broth
1 bay leaf
¼ teaspoon dried thyme

Mix flour and pepper. Dredge chicken breasts in flour mixture, coating on all sides. In a large, heavy frying pan, preheat olive oil over medium heat for 1 to 2 minutes. Place chicken in pan and cook on one side until golden brown. Turn pieces over and add garlic cloves and mushrooms to pan. Cook an additional 3 to 4 minutes, stirring gently for even heating but not turning chicken over again.

In a small bowl, combine balsamic vinegar, chicken broth, bay leaf, and thyme. Pour over chicken in pan; cover and cook over medium–low heat, stirring occasionally, until chicken is fork tender. Remove and discard bay leaf and garlic cloves. Remove chicken and keep warm. Continue cooking liquid in pan, stirring frequently, until it thickens to desired consistency. Pour sauce and mushrooms over chicken. Makes 4 servings.

NUTRITION (PER SERVING): 346 CALORIES

TOTAL FAT	7 g	(18% OF CALORIES)
PROTEIN	58 g	(67% OF CALORIES)
CARBOHYDRATES	13 g	(15% OF CALORIES)
CHOLESTEROL	137 mg	
SODIUM	432 mg	

Oven-Fried Chicken

½ cup dry bread crumbs
½ teaspoon Italian seasoning
½ teaspoon garlic salt
1 pound skinless boneless chicken breast halves
3 tablespoons light mayonnaise

Preheat oven to 425 degrees F. Combine bread crumbs, Italian seasoning, and garlic salt. Brush chicken pieces on all sides with mayonnaise and roll in seasoned bread crumbs to coat thoroughly. Spray broiler pan rack with nonstick cooking spray; arrange chicken pieces on rack. Bake for 15 to 20 minutes or until chicken is fork tender and juices run clear. Makes 4 servings.

NUTRITION (PER SERVING): 193 CALORIES

TOTAL FAT	4 g	(19% OF CALORIES)
PROTEIN	28 g	(58% OF CALORIES)
CARBOHYDRATES	11 g	(23% OF CALORIES)
CHOLESTEROL	69 mg	
SODIUM	222 mg	

Zesty Grilled Turkey

1½ pounds skinless boneless turkey breast tenders
1 cup nonfat plain yogurt
¼ cup lemon juice
3 tablespoons vegetable oil
¼ cup minced fresh parsley
¼ cup chopped green onions
2 cloves garlic, minced
2 teaspoons dill
½ teaspoon rosemary
½ teaspoon salt
¼ teaspoon pepper

Place turkey in a shallow glass baking dish. Combine remaining ingredients and spread over the turkey. Cover and refrigerate at least 6 hours (or overnight, if desired). Remove turkey, reserving marinade. Grill turkey, covered, over medium–hot coals, basting often with marinade, for 60 to 70 minutes or until juices run clear or internal temperature reaches 170 degrees F. Makes 6 servings.

NUTRITION (PER SERVING): 220 CALORIES

TOTAL FAT	9 g	(36% OF CALORIES)
PROTEIN	29 g	(54% OF CALORIES)
CARBOHYDRATES	5 g	(10% OF CALORIES)
CHOLESTEROL	67 mg	
SODIUM	289 mg	

Turkey Tacos

1 pound ground turkey
¼ cup chopped onions
1 package taco seasoning mix
¾ cup water
8 taco shells
2 cups shredded lettuce
2 tomatoes, chopped
¼ cup shredded reduced-fat cheddar cheese
Taco sauce
Nonfat sour cream

Spray a large frying pan with nonstick cooking spray and preheat 1 to 2 minutes over medium heat. Cook turkey and onions in preheated pan, stirring constantly, until turkey is browned and crumbly and onions are tender. Add taco seasoning mix and water; mix well. Heat to simmering point and simmer, uncovered, until mixture reaches desired consistency, about 5 minutes.

Warm taco shells in microwave or conventional oven. Spoon turkey mixture into shells and top with lettuce, tomatoes, and cheese. Serve with taco sauce and nonfat sour cream, if desired. Makes 8 servings.

NUTRITION (PER SERVING): 144 CALORIES

TOTAL FAT	7 g	(41% OF CALORIES)
PROTEIN	8 g	(22% OF CALORIES)
CARBOHYDRATES	14 g	(37% OF CALORIES)
CHOLESTEROL	25 mg	
SODIUM	471 mg	

Turkey Vegetable Skillet

1 pound ground turkey
1 small onion, chopped
1 clove garlic, minced
3 medium tomatoes, chopped
1 small zucchini, diced
¼ cup chopped dill pickle
1 teaspoon basil
½ teaspoon pepper

Spray a large frying pan with nonstick cooking spray. Add turkey, onions, and garlic; cook, stirring constantly, over medium-high heat until turkey is browned and crumbly. Stir in tomatoes, zucchini, pickle, basil, and pepper. Reduce heat and simmer, uncovered, for 5 to 10 minutes or until zucchini is tender. Serve with rice, or wrapped in a flour tortilla and garnished with salsa and nonfat sour cream. Makes 6 servings.

NUTRITION (PER SERVING): 138 CALORIES

TOTAL FAT	7 g	(43% OF CALORIES)
PROTEIN	15 g	(42% OF CALORIES)
CARBOHYDRATES	5 g	(14% OF CALORIES)
CHOLESTEROL	55 mg	
SODIUM	154 mg	

Sour Cream Turkey Patties

1 pound ground turkey
1 cup soft bread crumbs, divided
3 tablespoons light sour cream
⅓ cup skim milk
¼ teaspoon pepper
⅛ teaspoon nutmeg
1 tablespoon butter or margarine

Combine turkey, ½ cup bread crumbs, sour cream, milk, pepper, and nutmeg. Divide mixture in fourths and mold each portion into a flat patty. Spread remaining ½ cup bread crumbs on a plate; carefully dip patties in crumbs, covering on both sides. Place a cooking rack in a shallow baking dish; set patties on rack and let stand uncovered in refrigerator for 20 minutes. Spray a large frying pan with nonstick cooking spray. Melt butter or margarine in pan over medium heat. Add patties and brown 5 minutes on each side. Makes 4 servings.

NUTRITION (PER SERVING): 303 CALORIES

TOTAL FAT	13 g	(39% OF CALORIES)
PROTEIN	25 g	(33% OF CALORIES)
CARBOHYDRATES	21 g	(28% OF CALORIES)
CHOLESTEROL	94 mg	
SODIUM	336 mg	

Turkey Chili-Mac

1 package (8 ounces) elbow macaroni
1 pound ground turkey
½ cup chopped onions
¼ cup chopped green bell peppers
1 clove garlic, minced
2 cups low-sodium tomato juice
1 can (8 ounces) tomato sauce
1 teaspoon chili powder
1 teaspoon cumin
½ teaspoon salt
1 can (16 ounces) red kidney beans, undrained

Cook macaroni according to package directions, but omitting any salt or fat. Drain well and set aside.

Spray a large pot with nonstick cooking spray. Add turkey and cook over medium heat, stirring constantly, until browned and crumbly. Add onions, green peppers, and garlic. Cook, stirring constantly, for 5 minutes or until vegetables are tender. Stir in tomato juice, tomato sauce, chili powder, cumin, and salt. Bring to a boil. Reduce heat, cover, and simmer 20 minutes, stirring occasionally. Add kidney beans and cooked macaroni. Simmer uncovered an additional 15 minutes, stirring occasionally. Makes 8 servings.

NUTRITION (PER SERVING): 254 CALORIES

TOTAL FAT	5 g	(18% OF CALORIES)
PROTEIN	18 g	(28% OF CALORIES)
CARBOHYDRATES	35 g	(55% OF CALORIES)
CHOLESTEROL	41 mg	
SODIUM	559 mg	

Turkey Chili with Corn Bread Topping

1 pound ground turkey, cooked until crumbly
3 cups water
1 cup chopped onions
1 cup chopped green bell peppers
2 cans (14½ ounces each) stewed tomatoes, undrained
1 can (16 ounces) red kidney beans, drained
1 package (10 ounces) frozen corn
1 can (6 ounces) tomato paste
2 tablespoons chili powder
1 teaspoon oregano
¼ teaspoon salt
¼ teaspoon pepper
⅔ cup flour
⅔ cup stone-ground yellow cornmeal
2 teaspoons baking powder
¼ teaspoon salt
2 tablespoons light butter or margarine, cut into small pieces and chilled
2 tablespoons minced fresh parsley
⅔ cup skim milk

Spray a large kettle with nonstick cooking spray. In kettle, combine cooked turkey, water, onions, green peppers, tomatoes, beans, corn, tomato paste, chili powder, oregano, salt, and pepper. Bring to a boil over medium-high heat, stirring occasionally. Reduce heat and simmer uncovered for 30 minutes.

In a medium bowl, combine flour, cornmeal, baking powder, and salt. Using a fork or a pastry blender, mix in butter or margarine until mixture is the consistency of coarse meal. Stir in parsley. Make a well in the center of the mixture. Pour milk into well and stir just until moistened. Drop by spoonfuls onto hot chili. Simmer uncovered about 10 minutes; then cover and simmer 10 minutes more or until topping is set. Makes 6 servings.

NUTRITION (PER SERVING): 470 CALORIES

TOTAL FAT	10 g	(19% OF CALORIES)
PROTEIN	29 g	(25% OF CALORIES)
CARBOHYDRATES	66 g	(56% OF CALORIES)
CHOLESTEROL	52 mg	
SODIUM	1036 mg	

Marinated Turkey Breast

3 pounds skinless boneless turkey breast tenders
1 cup light soy sauce
1 cup vegetable oil
2 cups carbonated lemon-lime beverage
½ teaspoon horseradish (more or less to taste)
¼ teaspoon garlic

Cut turkey breast into pieces ½-inch to 1-inch thick. Arrange pieces in a large glass baking pan. Combine soy sauce, oil, lemon-lime beverage, horseradish, and garlic. Pour marinade over turkey, cover, and refrigerate for 3 to 4 hours (or overnight, if desired), turning pieces over occasionally. Remove from marinade and grill on barbecue 2 to 3 minutes on each side or until juices run clear. (Turkey may also be cooked in broiler; broil 4 to 6 inches from heat.) Makes 12 servings.

NUTRITION (PER SERVING): 149 CALORIES

TOTAL FAT	5 g	(30% OF CALORIES)
PROTEIN	25 g	(67% OF CALORIES)
CARBOHYDRATES	1 g	(3% OF CALORIES)
CHOLESTEROL	68 mg	
SODIUM	153 mg	

Slow-Cooked Cranberry Orange Relish

2 cups sugar
1 cup orange juice
1 teaspoon grated orange peel
4 cups fresh or frozen cranberries

Combine sugar, orange juice, and orange peel in a slow cooker. Stir until sugar is dissolved. Stir in the cranberries. Cover and cook on low setting for 6 to 8 hours. Pour mixture into a large bowl and mash with a potato masher. Cover and refrigerate several hours or overnight. (The longer this relish sits, the better it is.) Serve with chicken or turkey dishes. Makes 12 servings, ¼ cup each.

NUTRITION (PER SERVING): 161 CALORIES

TOTAL FAT	0 g	(1% OF CALORIES)
PROTEIN	0 g	(1% OF CALORIES)
CARBOHYDRATES	40 g	(99% OF CALORIES)
CHOLESTEROL	0 mg	
SODIUM	1 mg	

Caribbean Chicken

2 tablespoons vegetable oil
½ cup sliced green onions
1 red bell pepper, chopped
2 cloves garlic, finely chopped
1 teaspoon thyme
1 teaspoon curry powder
½ teaspoon salt
½ teaspoon cumin
½ teaspoon ginger
¼ teaspoon paprika
¼ teaspoon freshly ground black pepper
⅛ teaspoon cayenne pepper
1½ pounds skinless boneless chicken breast halves

Preheat oil in a medium frying pan. Add green onions, bell peppers, garlic, thyme, curry powder, salt, cumin, ginger, paprika, black pepper, and cayenne pepper. Cook over medium-high heat, stirring frequently, until bell pepper is tender-crisp. Cool to room temperature.

Arrange chicken breasts in a shallow glass baking dish and pour vegetable-spice mixture over top. Turn chicken to coat evenly. Cover and refrigerate at least 30 minutes but no longer than 3 hours, turning chicken pieces occasionally.

Remove chicken from marinade and discard marinade. Grill chicken 4 to 6 inches from coals for 15 to 20 minutes, turning occasionally. Shut grill lid while cooking. Chicken is ready when juices run clear and meat is no longer pink at thickest point. Makes 6 servings.

NUTRITION (PER SERVING): 171 CALORIES

TOTAL FAT	6 g	(32% OF CALORIES)
PROTEIN	27 g	(62% OF CALORIES)
CARBOHYDRATES	2 g	(6% OF CALORIES)
CHOLESTEROL	66 mg	
SODIUM	272 mg	

Turkey and Sausage Skillet

½ pound lean sausage meat
½ pound ground turkey
1 onion, chopped
1 clove garlic, pressed
1 teaspoon cumin
1 teaspoon oregano
⅛ teaspoon red pepper
2 cups water
1 package (10 ounces) frozen
   chopped spinach, thawed
1 package (6½ ounces) wild and
   long-grain rice mix
1 cup chopped dates

In a large, nonstick skillet, combine sausage, turkey, onion, and garlic. Cook, stirring frequently over medium-high heat until meat is crumbly and onion is translucent. Stir in cumin, oregano, and red pepper. Add water, spinach, and rice mix with its seasoning packet, and bring to a boil. Cover skillet, reduce heat, and simmer about 15 minutes, until liquid is absorbed and rice is tender. Stir in dates and heat through.

NUTRITION (PER SERVING): 221 CALORIES

TOTAL FAT	9 g	(35% OF CALORIES)
PROTEIN	10 g	(19% OF CALORIES)
CARBOHYDRATES	26 g	(47% OF CALORIES)
CHOLESTEROL	36 mg	
SODIUM	392 mg	

FISH AND SEAFOOD

Lime-Baked Fish Fillets

¼ cup lime juice
2 tablespoons light margarine
½ teaspoon dried parsley flakes
¼ teaspoon salt
1 clove garlic, minced
⅛ teaspoon pepper
4 white fish fillets (flounder, turbot, or orange roughy), about ¼ pound each

Preheat oven to 400 degrees F. Spray a 13 x 9-inch baking dish with nonstick cooking spray; set aside. In a small saucepan, combine lime juice, margarine, parsley, salt, garlic, and pepper. Cook over medium heat, stirring frequently, until margarine is melted. Arrange fish fillets in prepared dish and pour lime sauce over them. Bake for 20 to 25 minutes or until the fish flakes easily when tested with a fork. Serve immediately. Makes 4 servings.

NUTRITION (PER SERVING): 218 CALORIES

TOTAL FAT	7 g	(29% OF CALORIES)
PROTEIN	37 g	(67% OF CALORIES)
CARBOHYDRATES	2 g	(3% OF CALORIES)
CHOLESTEROL	110 mg	
SODIUM	346 mg	

Arctic Halibut

Pictured on cover.

2 pounds halibut fillets
2 tablespoons lemon juice
½ cup light sour cream
½ cup light mayonnaise
½ cup green onions, chopped fine
1 teaspoon garlic salt, divided
¼ teaspoon Worcestershire sauce
1 cup soft bread crumbs
1 tablespoon light butter or margarine, melted

Arrange halibut fillets in a large glass baking dish. Sprinkle lemon juice over fillets. Mix together sour cream, mayonnaise, green onions, ½ teaspoon garlic salt, and Worcestershire sauce. Spread over halibut fillets. Toss bread crumbs with ½ teaspoon garlic salt and melted butter or margarine. Sprinkle crumbs over halibut. Bake at 350 degrees F. for 25 to 30 minutes or until fish flakes easily with fork. Do not overbake. Makes 6 servings.

NUTRITION (PER SERVING): 273 CALORIES

TOTAL FAT	10 g	(30% OF CALORIES)
PROTEIN	35 g	(52% OF CALORIES)
CARBOHYDRATES	12 g	(18% OF CALORIES)
CHOLESTEROL	58 mg	
SODIUM	270 mg	

Broiled Cod Fillets

4 pounds cod fillets (8 fillets)
1 teaspoon salt
1 teaspoon paprika
¼ cup lemon juice
¼ cup light butter, melted
¼ cup chopped fresh parsley

Wash fillets well under cold running water. Spray broiler pan rack with nonstick cooking spray. Place fillets on rack; sprinkle with salt and paprika. Drizzle lemon juice and melted butter over fish. Broil about 6 inches from heat for approximately 10 minutes for each 1 inch thickness, turning once and basting with lemon and melted butter. Garnish with parsley and serve immediately. Makes 8 servings.

NUTRITION (PER SERVING): 202 CALORIES

TOTAL FAT	5 g	(20% OF CALORIES)
PROTEIN	39 g	(77% OF CALORIES)
CARBOHYDRATES	1 g	(2% OF CALORIES)
CHOLESTEROL	101 mg	
SODIUM	464 mg	

Baked Fish with Seafood Sauce

1 pound white fish fillets (flounder, turbot,
*   or orange roughy), cut into 8 pieces*
½ cup low-sodium chicken broth
¼ teaspoon white pepper, divided
3½ teaspoons light margarine, divided
½ cup chopped fresh mushrooms
¼ cup finely chopped onions
2 tablespoons flour
1 cup evaporated skim milk
¼ teaspoon salt
½ pound imitation crab, drained and flaked
¼ cup shredded reduced-fat Monterey Jack cheese

Preheat oven to 350 degrees F. Place fish in a single layer in a glass baking dish. Pour chicken broth over fillets and sprinkle with ⅛ teaspoon white pepper. Bake for 20 minutes or until fish flakes easily with a fork.

While fish is cooking, melt 2 teaspoons of the margarine in a frying pan. Add mushrooms and onions and cook over medium heat, stirring constantly, until tender. Set aside. In a heavy saucepan over low heat, melt remaining 1½ teaspoons margarine. Add flour and stir to make a smooth paste. Cook and stir for 1 minute. Raise heat to medium and stir in milk. Continue cooking, stirring constantly, until mixture thickens and bubbles. Stir in mushroom mixture, salt, ⅛ teaspoon white pepper, and imitation crab. Remove from heat and set aside.

Remove fish from oven. Carefully lift fillets from baking dish and place in individual flameproof bowls. Spoon about 2 tablespoons sauce over each portion; sprinkle with cheese. Return fish to oven and bake 5 minutes longer or until hot and bubbly. Makes 8 servings.

NUTRITION (PER SERVING): 137 CALORIES

TOTAL FAT	4 g	(24% OF CALORIES)
PROTEIN	17 g	(50% OF CALORIES)
CARBOHYDRATES	9 g	(26% OF CALORIES)
CHOLESTEROL	34 mg	
SODIUM	509 mg	

Easy Fish and Rice Bake

1 tablespoon light butter
¾ cup chopped onions
½ cup chopped celery
1 clove garlic, minced
½ cup uncooked long-grain rice
2 cans (14½ ounces each) chopped
  stewed tomatoes, undrained
1 teaspoon lemon pepper
½ teaspoon salt
⅛ teaspoon cayenne pepper (optional)
1 pound white fish fillets
¼ cup chopped fresh parsley

Preheat oven to 400 degrees F. In a large skillet, heat butter over medium heat. Sauté onions, celery, and garlic in butter until tender. Stir in rice and sauté about 5 minutes, or until rice browns slightly. Add tomatoes with liquid, lemon pepper, salt, and cayenne pepper. Place fish in a single layer in a shallow glass baking dish. Spoon rice mixture over fish. Cover with foil. Bake for 45 to 50 minutes or until rice is tender. Allow to stand 5 minutes before serving. Sprinkle with parsley. Makes 6 servings.

NUTRITION (PER SERVING):   148 CALORIES

TOTAL FAT	3 g	(16% OF CALORIES)
PROTEIN	15 g	(40% OF CALORIES)
CARBOHYDRATES	16 g	(44% OF CALORIES)
CHOLESTEROL	36 mg	
SODIUM	437 mg	

Sour Cream Halibut Steaks

2 pounds halibut steaks
1 teaspoon salt
¼ teaspoon pepper
¾ cup nonfat sour cream
¼ cup dry bread crumbs
¼ teaspoon garlic powder
1½ teaspoons chopped fresh chives
¼ cup Parmesan cheese
1 teaspoon paprika

Place halibut steaks close together in a shallow baking dish sprayed with nonstick cooking spray. Sprinkle with salt and pepper. Mix together sour cream, bread crumbs, garlic powder, and chives and spread over steaks. Sprinkle with Parmesan cheese and paprika. Bake uncovered at 400 degrees F. for 15 to 20 minutes or until fish flakes easily. Makes 8 servings.

NUTRITION (PER SERVING):   174 CALORIES

TOTAL FAT	5 g	(26% OF CALORIES)
PROTEIN	27 g	(61% OF CALORIES)
CARBOHYDRATES	6 g	(13% OF CALORIES)
CHOLESTEROL	42 mg	
SODIUM	451 mg	

Microwaved Fillets with Red Potatoes

⅓ cup water

3 tablespoons lemon juice

½ teaspoon chicken bouillon granules

4 red potatoes, scrubbed and thinly sliced

2 tablespoons finely chopped green onions

4 white fish fillets (flounder, turbot, or orange roughy), about ¼ pound each

¼ teaspoon salt

⅛ teaspoon pepper

Combine water, lemon juice, and bouillon and stir until bouillon is completely dissolved. Spray a 9-inch square baking dish with nonstick cooking spray and pour mixture into it. Layer potato slices over liquid. Cover dish with plastic wrap; make 2 or 3 small slits in wrap to vent. Microwave on high power for 8 to 10 minutes, rotating dish after 5 minutes. Sprinkle green onions over potatoes; replace cover and microwave on high power for 1 minute more.

Add fish to baking dish and sprinkle with salt and pepper. Spoon liquid from dish over the top of the fillets. Cover with plastic wrap and microwave on high power for 8 to 10 minutes, rotating dish after 5 minutes. Fish is done if it flakes easily with a fork. Let stand, covered, for 2 minutes; then serve immediately. Makes 4 servings.

NUTRITION (PER SERVING): 263 CALORIES

TOTAL FAT	8 g	(20% OF CALORIES)
PROTEIN	20 g	(24% OF CALORIES)
CARBOHYDRATES	27 g	(55% OF CALORIES)
CHOLESTEROL	23 mg	
SODIUM	266 mg	

Oven-Fried Fish

1 egg white

3 tablespoons frozen orange juice concentrate, thawed

1 tablespoon Worcestershire sauce

½ cup crushed soda crackers (about 12 crackers)

¼ cup toasted wheat germ

1 pound sole or flounder fillets

1 tablespoon butter or margarine, melted

In a small bowl, beat together the egg white, orange juice concentrate, and Worcestershire sauce. In a separate dish, stir together the crushed crackers and wheat germ.

Dip fish fillets in the egg white mixture, then in the crumb mixture. Arrange fillets in a 9-inch square baking dish and drizzle with melted butter or margarine. Preheat oven to 500 degrees F. Bake fillets for 8 to 10 minutes or until fish flakes easily with a fork. Makes 4 servings.

NUTRITION (PER SERVING): 212 CALORIES

TOTAL FAT	6 g	(24% OF CALORIES)
PROTEIN	24 g	(45% OF CALORIES)
CARBOHYDRATES	16 g	(31% OF CALORIES)
CHOLESTEROL	57 mg	
SODIUM	231 mg	

Fat-Free Tartar Sauce

½ cup nonfat mayonnaise

1 tablespoon lemon juice

½ teaspoon dried minced onions

1 tablespoon sweet pickle relish

Mix all ingredients together. Chill to blend flavors. Makes 4 servings, about 2 tablespoons each.

NUTRITION (PER SERVING): 30 CALORIES

TOTAL FAT	0 g	(1% OF CALORIES)
PROTEIN	0 g	(1% OF CALORIES)
CARBOHYDRATES	7 g	(99% OF CALORIES)
CHOLESTEROL	0 mg	
SODIUM	381 mg	

Sesame Fillets

2 teaspoons tomato paste
2 teaspoons Dijon-style mustard
½ teaspoon tarragon
¼ cup nonfat buttermilk
1 pound white fish fillets (sole, flounder, turbot, or orange roughy)
2 tablespoons flour
3½ tablespoons sesame seeds
4 teaspoons vegetable oil

Mix together the tomato paste, mustard, and tarragon. Coat the fish fillets thoroughly with buttermilk, then spread on both sides with the tomato paste mixture. Stir together the flour and sesame seeds and spread in a shallow dish or pan. Place the fillets in the flour mixture and press to coat fish on both sides. Refrigerate fillets uncovered on a rack for 30 minutes to set the coating.

Preheat the vegetable oil in a large heavy frying pan over medium-high heat. Place the fillets in the pan and cook until golden brown, about 1½ to 2 minutes on each side. Watch the sesame seeds carefully, and reduce heat if they brown too quickly. Fish is done if it flakes easily with a fork. Serve immediately. Makes 4 servings.

NUTRITION (PER SERVING): 119 CALORIES

TOTAL FAT	9 g	(71% OF CALORIES)
PROTEIN	3 g	(11% OF CALORIES)
CARBOHYDRATES	5 g	(18% OF CALORIES)
CHOLESTEROL	1 mg	
SODIUM	53 mg	

Overnight Marinated Halibut

2 pounds halibut steaks
1 small bottle (8 ounces) light Italian dressing

Cut halibut into 6 serving-size pieces. Put fish into a heavy-duty plastic zip-lock bag and add dressing. Marinate overnight in refrigerator, turning bag occasionally. Remove fish from marinade and grill on barbecue or bake on broiler pan in oven set to 350 degrees F. until fish flakes easily with a fork, about 20 minutes. Do not overcook, as it will dry out fish. Makes 6 servings.

Note: Salmon is also delicious prepared this way.

NUTRITION (PER SERVING): 204 CALORIES

TOTAL FAT	7 g	(33% OF CALORIES)
PROTEIN	32 g	(63% OF CALORIES)
CARBOHYDRATES	2 g	(4% OF CALORIES)
CHOLESTEROL	52 mg	
SODIUM	398 mg	

Salmon Patties

1 tablespoon margarine
½ cup finely chopped onions
1 can (14½ ounces) red salmon, undrained
2 egg whites, slightly beaten
1 cup uncooked, unprocessed oat bran
1 teaspoon prepared mustard
¼ teaspoon salt
¾ cup fine dry bread crumbs
1 tablespoon vegetable oil

Melt margarine in a small frying pan; add onions and sauté until translucent. Place undrained salmon in a medium bowl. Remove skin and bones. Mash well with a fork to blend salmon with liquid from can. Mix in the onions, egg whites, oat bran, mustard, and salt, stirring to combine thoroughly. Mold into 6 patties. Dip patties in bread crumbs, coating on both sides.

In a large frying pan, preheat oil over medium heat. Cook patties in heated oil until evenly browned, about 5 minutes on each side. Drain on paper towels. Makes 6 servings.

NUTRITION (PER SERVING): 208 CALORIES

TOTAL FAT	8 g	(35% OF CALORIES)
PROTEIN	19 g	(37% OF CALORIES)
CARBOHYDRATES	15 g	(28% OF CALORIES)
CHOLESTEROL	36 mg	
SODIUM	262 mg	

Seafood Casserole

1 tablespoon margarine
2 cups sliced fresh mushrooms
1 green bell pepper, chopped
½ cup chopped onions
½ cup chopped celery
¾ pound peeled and deveined medium-size shrimp
½ cup crabmeat, drained and flaked
1 cup evaporated skim milk
1 cup chicken broth
¼ cup flour
2 cups cooked brown rice
1½ cups cooked wild rice
2 teaspoons lemon juice
4 drops bottled hot pepper sauce
¼ teaspoon dried parsley flakes
¼ teaspoon salt
⅛ teaspoon pepper
¼ cup dry bread crumbs

Melt margarine in a large frying pan over medium-high heat. Add mushrooms, green pepper, onions, and celery and sauté until onions are translucent and vegetables are tender-crisp. Add shrimp and crabmeat; stir-fry until shrimp turn pink, about 5 minutes. Set aside.

In a large saucepan, combine milk with chicken broth. Gradually whisk in the flour, beating until smooth. Stirring constantly, cook over medium heat until mixture thickens.

Remove from heat and stir in shrimp mixture, brown and wild rice, lemon juice, hot pepper sauce, parsley, salt, and pepper. Spoon mixture into a 2-quart glass baking dish; sprinkle with bread crumbs. Bake at 400 degrees F. for 30 minutes or until bubbly and heated through. Makes 8 servings.

NUTRITION (PER SERVING): 231 CALORIES

TOTAL FAT	3 g	(13% OF CALORIES)
PROTEIN	17 g	(30% OF CALORIES)
CARBOHYDRATES	33 g	(57% OF CALORIES)
CHOLESTEROL	71 mg	
SODIUM	431 MG	

Tuna Salad

1 unpeeled Red Delicious apple
1 can (6 ounces) solid white tuna in water
1 hard-cooked egg white, chopped fine
¼ cup light mayonnaise
2 tablespoons diced celery
1 tablespoon sweet pickle relish
½ teaspoon lemon juice
Lettuce leaves

Cut apple in half and remove seeds and core. Set one half aside, and chop the other half fine. Drain tuna well; place in a medium bowl and flake with fork. Add chopped apple, egg white, mayonnaise, celery, pickle relish, and lemon juice; mix well. Cover and let stand in refrigerator at least 2 hours to blend flavors. To serve, place lettuce leaves on individual salad plates and top each with a scoop of salad. Slice remaining apple half and use as garnish. Makes 4 servings.

NUTRITION (PER SERVING): 133 CALORIES

TOTAL FAT	4 g	(28% OF CALORIES)
PROTEIN	12 g	(37% OF CALORIES)
CARBOHYDRATES	12 g	(35% OF CALORIES)
CHOLESTEROL	21 mg	
SODIUM	285 mg	

Salmon Salad

1 can (14½ ounces) salmon
½ cup chopped green bell peppers
½ cup diced celery
¼ cup chopped dill pickles
¼ cup light mayonnaise
2 tablespoons lemon juice

Drain salmon thoroughly and remove skin and bones. Flake salmon with a fork. In a medium bowl combine salmon, green peppers, celery, and pickles. Stir in mayonnaise and lemon juice; mix well. Cover and let stand in refrigerator 2 hours to blend flavors. Serve as a sandwich or a salad. Makes 5 servings.

NUTRITION (PER SERVING): 155 CALORIES

TOTAL FAT	8 g	(45% OF CALORIES)
PROTEIN	18 g	(46% OF CALORIES)
CARBOHYDRATES	4 g	(10% OF CALORIES)
CHOLESTEROL	51 mg	
SODIUM	653 mg	

Salmon Teriyaki

¼ cup light soy sauce
¼ cup water
¼ cup sugar
1 teaspoon grated fresh ginger root
1 tablespoon cornstarch
1 tablespoon water
¼ cup celery
¼ cup chopped onions
4 salmon steaks, about ¼ pound each
1 lemon, sliced

In a small saucepan, combine soy sauce, ¼ cup water, sugar, and grated ginger. Bring to a boil. Dissolve cornstarch in 1 tablespoon water and add to soy sauce mixture. Cook until thickened (it will not be very thick). Add celery and onions. Arrange salmon steaks in a glass baking dish; pour sauce over steaks and place lemon slices on top. Bake at 350 degrees F. for 20 to 30 minutes or until fish flakes easily with fork. Baste several times during baking. Makes 4 servings.

Note: Fish can also be marinated in the sauce for 30 minutes or more and then broiled or cooked on a barbecue grill. Baste several times during cooking.

NUTRITION (PER SERVING): 238 CALORIES

TOTAL FAT	6 g	(23% OF CALORIES)
PROTEIN	28 g	(47% OF CALORIES)
CARBOHYDRATES	18 g	(30% OF CALORIES)
CHOLESTEROL	112 mg	
SODIUM	925 mg	

Shrimp Creole with Rice

1 tablespoon olive oil
½ cup chopped green bell peppers
½ cup chopped green onions
1 cup chopped celery
2 tablespoons flour
⅛ teaspoon paprika
2 cans (14½ ounces each) whole stewed tomatoes
1 bay leaf
2 cans (5 ounces each) shrimp, drained,
    or 1½ pounds fresh cooked shrimp
1 tablespoon chopped fresh parsley
½ teaspoon salt
3 cups hot cooked rice
2 teaspoons light butter or margarine

Heat oil in large frying pan. Add green peppers, onions, and celery; sauté until soft but not brown (5 to 10 minutes on low heat). Add flour and paprika; blend well. Drain tomatoes, reserving liquid and adding water if needed to measure 2 cups. Add tomato liquid to vegetables in frying pan; cook over medium heat, stirring constantly, until smooth and thick. Chop tomatoes slightly and add to vegetable mixture. Add bay leaf. Cover and simmer 30 minutes. Add shrimp and continue cooking until shrimp is heated (about 5 minutes). Add parsley and salt. Stir light butter or margarine into hot rice and serve shrimp mixture over rice. Makes 6 servings.

NUTRITION (PER SERVING): 474 CALORIES

TOTAL FAT	4 g	(7% OF CALORIES)
PROTEIN	19 g	(16% OF CALORIES)
CARBOHYDRATES	91 g	(77% OF CALORIES)
CHOLESTEROL	92 mg	
SODIUM	841 mg	

Basil Shrimp and Broccoli

1 tablespoon vegetable oil
¾ pound peeled and deveined medium-size shrimp
2 cups fresh chopped broccoli
1 red bell pepper, cut into thin strips
½ cup snow peas
½ cup fresh sliced mushrooms
¼ cup sliced water chestnuts
2 teaspoons chicken bouillon granules
½ cup boiling water
¼ cup cold water
1 tablespoon cornstarch
1 teaspoon basil
1 teaspoon lemon juice
½ cup sliced green onions

In a large frying pan over medium heat, preheat oil for about 1 minute. Stir-fry shrimp in hot oil until they turn pink, about 4 minutes. Remove shrimp and set aside. Leave frying pan on heat and add broccoli, red pepper strips, snow peas, mushrooms, and water chestnuts. Stir-fry until tender-crisp.

Dissolve bouillon granules in boiling water; add to vegetables in pan. Combine cold water, cornstarch, basil, and lemon juice and stir until smooth. Gradually pour into vegetable mixture, stirring constantly over medium heat until thickened. Add green onions and shrimp; heat through. Makes 4 servings.

NUTRITION (PER SERVING): 177 CALORIES

TOTAL FAT	5 g	(27% OF CALORIES)
PROTEIN	21 g	(47% OF CALORIES)
CARBOHYDRATES	12 g	(26% OF CALORIES)
CHOLESTEROL	129 mg	
SODIUM	265 mg	

Cajun Seafood Linguine

1 large onion, thinly sliced
1 cup chopped green bell peppers
2 cloves garlic, minced
2 cans (14½ ounces each) chopped stewed tomatoes, drained
1 cup low-sodium chicken broth
1 teaspoon basil
½ to 1 teaspoon Cajun seasoning (according to taste)
¼ teaspoon salt
2 bay leaves
⅔ pound small fresh shrimp, peeled and deveined
½ pound bay scallops
3 cups hot cooked linguine

Spray a large frying pan with nonstick cooking spray and preheat over medium heat on stove. Sauté onions, green peppers, and garlic in heated skillet until tender-crisp. Add tomatoes, chicken broth, basil, Cajun seasoning, salt, and bay leaves. Bring to a boil; reduce heat and simmer, uncovered for 10 minutes. Stir in shrimp and scallops. Cover and simmer until shrimp are pink and scallops are cooked, about 5 minutes. Remove and discard bay leaf. Serve seafood mixture over hot linguine. Makes 4 servings.

NUTRITION (PER SERVING): 367 CALORIES

TOTAL FAT	3 g	(7% OF CALORIES)
PROTEIN	40 g	(44% OF CALORIES)
CARBOHYDRATES	45 g	(49% OF CALORIES)
CHOLESTEROL	181 mg	
SODIUM	523 mg	

Shrimp and Pepper Stir Fry

2 tablespoons lime juice
2 teaspoons cornstarch
½ teaspoon cumin
¼ teaspoon salt
¼ teaspoon black pepper
1½ pounds large fresh shrimp, peeled and deveined
1½ cups chopped yellow bell peppers
1½ cups chopped red bell peppers
1 cup chopped red onions
⅓ cup low-sodium chicken broth
2 cloves garlic, chopped fine
⅛ teaspoon cayenne pepper
2 tablespoons chopped fresh cilantro

Combine lime juice, cornstarch, cumin, salt, and black pepper in a glass bowl; mix well. Add shrimp; stir to coat thoroughly. Cover and marinate in refrigerator for 1 hour.

Spray a large frying pan with nonstick cooking spray and preheat over medium heat. Add yellow and red bell peppers, onions, chicken broth, garlic, and cayenne pepper. Cook, stirring constantly, for 2 minutes. Add shrimp with marinade and cook an additional 3 to 4 minutes, stirring constantly, until shrimp turn pink. Sprinkle with cilantro. Makes 6 servings.

NUTRITION (PER SERVING): 148 CALORIES

TOTAL FAT	1 g	(9% OF CALORIES)
PROTEIN	25 g	(67% OF CALORIES)
CARBOHYDRATES	9 g	(24% OF CALORIES)
CHOLESTEROL	221 mg	
SODIUM	359 mg	

Shrimp Fettuccine

2 tablespoons margarine
1 cup sliced fresh mushrooms
¼ cup chopped green onions
2 cloves garlic, minced
1 pound medium fresh shrimp, peeled and deveined
1 package (8 ounces) fettuccine
¾ cup grated Romano cheese
¾ cup grated Parmesan cheese
¾ cup skim milk
½ teaspoon salt
¼ cup chopped fresh parsley

Melt margarine in a large frying pan over medium heat; add mushrooms, onions, and garlic, and sauté for 10 minutes. Stir in shrimp and continue cooking, stirring constantly, until shrimp are pink, about 5 minutes. Remove from heat; cover and keep warm.

In a large saucepan, cook fettuccine according to package directions, leaving out salt and fat. Drain fettuccine and return it to the pan. Stir in the cheeses, milk, and salt; mix well. Add shrimp mixture and parsley, tossing gently to combine. Serve immediately. Makes 8 servings.

NUTRITION (PER SERVING): 239 CALORIES

TOTAL FAT	9 g	(33% OF CALORIES)
PROTEIN	21 g	(36% OF CALORIES)
CARBOHYDRATES	19 g	(31% OF CALORIES)
CHOLESTEROL	121 mg	
SODIUM	514 mg	

Tangy Orange Roughy with Almonds

4 teaspoons sliced almonds
2 teaspoons margarine
2 tablespoons minced fresh parsley
1 tablespoon grated lemon rind
3 tablespoons lemon juice
¼ teaspoon salt
1 pound orange roughy fillets

Spread almonds in a single layer in a shallow dish or pie pan; toast in 325 degree F. oven for 3 to 5 minutes, or until lightly browned. Set aside. In a small frying pan over low heat, melt margarine; add parsley, lemon rind, lemon juice, and salt. Cook, stirring frequently, until heated through. Remove from heat and set aside.

Prepare a broiler pan by covering it with aluminum foil and preheating it under the broiler for 3 minutes. Place fish fillets on preheated pan and brush with lemon mixture. Broil 6 inches from heat until fish flakes easily with a fork, about 8 minutes. Top fillets with toasted almonds. Makes 4 servings.

NUTRITION (PER SERVING): 181 CALORIES

TOTAL FAT	11 g	(56% OF CALORIES)
PROTEIN	17 g	(39% OF CALORIES)
CARBOHYDRATES	2 g	(5% OF CALORIES)
CHOLESTEROL	23 mg	
SODIUM	244 mg	

Broiled Fish with Tomato Topping

2 tablespoons chopped green onions
1 clove garlic, minced
1 teaspoon olive oil
2 tablespoons chopped fresh parsley
1 teaspoon basil
½ teaspoon salt
⅛ teaspoon pepper
2 small tomatoes, peeled and chopped
1 pound orange roughy fillets

In a medium frying pan over low heat, sauté green onions and garlic in olive oil until tender. Add parsley, basil, salt, and pepper and heat through. Remove from heat and stir in tomatoes. Set aside.

Prepare a broiler pan by covering it with aluminum foil and preheating it under the broiler for 3 minutes. Place fish fillets on preheated pan and broil 6 inches from heat for 5 minutes. Spoon tomato mixture over fillets; continue broiling until fish flakes easily with a fork, about 3 minutes. Makes 4 servings.

Note: This dish may be cooked on a grill by wrapping each portion in a double layer of aluminum foil. Cook until fish flakes easily with a fork, 8 to 10 minutes.

NUTRITION (PER SERVING): 161 CALORIES

TOTAL FAT	9 g	(52% OF CALORIES)
PROTEIN	17 g	(43% OF CALORIES)
CARBOHYDRATES	2 g	(6% OF CALORIES)
CHOLESTEROL	23 mg	
SODIUM	370 mg	

PASTA, BEANS, AND RICE

Pasta and Vegetable Carbonara

6 ounces bowtie or farfalle pasta
2 slices bacon
1 cup coarsely chopped red bell peppers
2 cups chopped broccoli florets
2 teaspoons flour
¼ teaspoon salt
¼ teaspoon pepper
¾ cup half and half
¼ cup grated Parmesan cheese

Cook pasta as directed on package. Drain and keep warm. In a large frying pan, cook bacon over medium heat until crisp. Drain, reserving 1 tablespoon drippings in the pan. Sauté bell pepper and broccoli in drippings for 3 to 5 minutes or until vegetables are tender-crisp. Crumble bacon. Add pasta and bacon to the vegetables in the pan and cook 3 to 5 minutes longer, stirring frequently. Combine flour, salt, pepper, and half and half in a small bowl. Whisk with a wire whisk until smooth. Add to mixture in skillet and cook, stirring constantly, until thickened. Add Parmesan cheese and stir. Makes 6 servings.

NUTRITION (PER SERVING): 196 CALORIES

TOTAL FAT	8 g	(37% OF CALORIES)
PROTEIN	7 g	(28% OF CALORIES)
CARBOHYDRATES	24 g	(49% OF CALORIES)
CHOLESTEROL	41 mg	
SODIUM	229 mg	

Fettuccine Alfredo Lite

1 package (8 ounces) fettuccine
1 tablespoon light margarine
2 cloves garlic, minced
1 cup evaporated skim milk
3 tablespoons grated Parmesan or Romano cheese
1 teaspoon basil
⅛ teaspoon nutmeg
¼ cup chopped fresh parsley
Freshly ground black pepper (optional)

Cook fettuccine as instructed on package, omitting any fat and salt. Drain. Return to pan and stir in margarine and garlic, mixing gently to coat pasta. Add milk, cheese, basil, and nutmeg. Cook, stirring constantly, over medium heat until just thickened, about 5 to 7 minutes. Sprinkle with chopped parsley and pepper, if desired. Serve immediately. Makes 6 servings.

NUTRITION (PER SERVING): 171 CALORIES

TOTAL FAT	3 g	(16% OF CALORIES)
PROTEIN	9 g	(21% OF CALORIES)
CARBOHYDRATES	27 g	(63% OF CALORIES)
CHOLESTEROL	31 mg	
SODIUM	115 mg	

Sausage Ravioli with Tomatoes

1 package refrigerated sausage-filled ravioli
1 tablespoon olive oil
1 medium yellow onion, cut in ¼-inch wedges
½ cup chopped green bell peppers
1 clove garlic, minced
1 can (14½ ounces) chopped stewed
    tomatoes, undrained
½ teaspoon basil
¼ teaspoon salt
1 dash cayenne pepper

Cook ravioli as directed on package. Drain and keep warm. In a large frying pan, heat oil over medium-high heat. Stir in onion, bell peppers, and garlic. Cook for 3 to 5 minutes or until vegetables are crisp-tender, stirring occasionally. Add tomatoes with liquid, basil, salt, and cayenne pepper. Bring to a boil. Reduce heat and simmer until sauce is slightly thickened, about 5 minutes. Add cooked ravioli and heat through, stirring frequently. Makes 4 servings.

NUTRITION (PER SERVING): 87 CALORIES

TOTAL FAT	4 g	(40% OF CALORIES)
PROTEIN	2 g	(8% OF CALORIES)
CARBOHYDRATES	11 g	(52% OF CALORIES)
CHOLESTEROL	0 mg	
SODIUM	159 mg	

Lasagna

1½ pounds extra-lean ground beef
1 clove garlic, minced
1 tablespoon dried parsley flakes
1 tablespoon basil
1 teaspoon salt
1 can (14½ ounces) stewed tomatoes, undrained
1 can (6 ounces) tomato paste
1 package (10 ounces) lasagna noodles
3 cups 1% low-fat cottage cheese
2 egg whites, beaten
½ teaspoon pepper
2 tablespoons dried parsley flakes
½ cup grated light Parmesan cheese
1 pound part-skim mozzarella cheese, thinly sliced

Brown ground beef in saucepan. Drain. Add garlic, parsley flakes, basil, and salt. Mix with tomatoes in juice and tomato paste. Simmer, uncovered, until thick, about one hour; stir occasionally. Cook lasagna noodles as directed on package; drain and rinse in cold water. Preheat oven to 375 degrees F. Mix cottage cheese with beaten egg whites, pepper, parsley flakes, and Parmesan cheese. Place half of the noodles in a 13 x 9-inch baking pan. Spoon on half the cottage cheese mixture. Next place a layer of sliced mozzarella cheese; then spoon on a layer of meat mixture. Repeat the layers, ending with layer of mozzarella on top. Bake, uncovered, for 30 minutes. Makes 15 servings.

NUTRITION (PER SERVING): 320 CALORIES

TOTAL FAT	15 g	(41% OF CALORIES)
PROTEIN	27 g	(33% OF CALORIES)
CARBOHYDRATES	21 g	(26% OF CALORIES)
CHOLESTEROL	53 mg	
SODIUM	676 mg	

Festive Potato Salad (page 98)

Asparagus Pasta

1 package (8 ounces) mostaccioli or penne noodles
1 pound fresh asparagus
2 cloves garlic, minced
½ teaspoon crushed red pepper flakes
2 dashes bottled hot pepper sauce
¼ cup olive oil
1 tablespoon butter or margarine
Salt to taste
¼ teaspoon pepper
¼ cup grated Parmesan cheese

Cook noodles according to directions on package, omitting any fat. Drain and set aside. Cut asparagus into 1½-inch pieces. Combine garlic, red pepper flakes, and hot pepper sauce with oil and butter or margarine in a frying pan; sauté over medium heat for 2 to 3 minutes. Stir in asparagus, salt, and pepper, and continue cooking, stirring frequently, until asparagus is tender–crisp, about 8 minutes. Place hot pasta in serving bowl. Pour asparagus over pasta and sprinkle with Parmesan cheese. Toss gently to combine. Makes 6 servings.

NUTRITION (PER SERVING): 263 CALORIES

TOTAL FAT	12 g	(41% OF CALORIES)
PROTEIN	9 g	(14% OF CALORIES)
CARBOHYDRATES	30 g	(45% OF CALORIES)
CHOLESTEROL	44 mg	
SODIUM	157 mg	

Mock Pasta Alfredo

1 package (8 ounces) spiral noodles
   or other pasta of choice
1½ cups 1% low-fat cottage cheese
½ cup skim milk
2 cloves garlic, minced
2 tablespoons flour
1 tablespoon lemon juice
1 teaspoon basil
½ teaspoon dry mustard
¼ teaspoon pepper
¼ teaspoon salt
1 large tomato, seeded and chopped

Cook pasta according to directions on package, omitting any fat. Drain well and set aside. Combine cottage cheese, milk, and garlic in the container of a blender or food processor. Blend until smooth. Add flour, lemon juice, basil, mustard, pepper, and salt and blend until thoroughly combined. Pour mixture into a large saucepan and cook, stirring constantly, over medium heat just until thickened. Place pasta in serving bowl; pour sauce over and top with chopped tomatoes. Serve immediately. Makes 4 servings.

NUTRITION (PER SERVING): 260 CALORIES

TOTAL FAT	3 g	(9% OF CALORIES)
PROTEIN	19 g	(29% OF CALORIES)
CARBOHYDRATES	40 g	(62% OF CALORIES)
CHOLESTEROL	46 mg	
SODIUM	526 mg	

Chunky Meatless Spaghetti

1 package (16 ounces) spaghetti noodles
2 tablespoons vegetable oil
3 cloves garlic, minced
½ cup chopped celery
½ cup chopped onions
1½ cups chopped zucchini
½ cup chopped green bell peppers
1 small can (2¼ ounces) sliced ripe olives, drained
2 teaspoons beef bouillon granules
½ cup hot water
1 can (4 ounces) sliced mushrooms, drained
1 can (14½ ounces) chopped stewed tomatoes, undrained
2 cans (8 ounces each) tomato sauce
1 can (6 ounces) tomato paste
1 tablespoon brown sugar
1 teaspoon basil
1 teaspoon oregano
1 teaspoon dried parsley flakes
½ teaspoon salt
¼ teaspoon pepper

Cook spaghetti according to package directions, omitting any fat. Drain well and set aside. Heat oil in a large saucepan; add garlic, celery, and onions and sauté over medium heat until onion is translucent. Stir in zucchini, green peppers, and olives; continue cooking, stirring frequently, for 2 to 3 minutes. Dissolve bouillon granules in hot water; add to vegetables. Add mushrooms, tomatoes with liquid, tomato sauce, tomato paste, brown sugar, basil, oregano, parsley flakes, salt, and pepper. Bring sauce to a boil. Reduce heat and simmer, covered, for 1 hour, stirring occasionally. Pour sauce over noodles and serve. Makes 8 servings.

NUTRITION (PER SERVING): 345 CALORIES

TOTAL FAT	5 g	(13% OF CALORIES)
PROTEIN	12 g	(13% OF CALORIES)
CARBOHYDRATES	64 g	(74% OF CALORIES)
CHOLESTEROL	0 mg	
SODIUM	563 mg	

Zucchini Lasagna

1 teaspoon olive oil
1 cup sliced fresh mushrooms
½ cup chopped onions
1 clove garlic, minced
2 cans (8 ounces each) tomato sauce
1 teaspoon basil
½ teaspoon sugar
½ teaspoon oregano
⅛ teaspoon pepper
6 lasagna noodles, cooked and drained
3 cups thinly sliced zucchini
2 cups 1% low-fat cottage cheese
½ cup grated Parmesan cheese
1 tablespoon flour
1 cup shredded part-skim mozzarella cheese

Heat oil in a medium frying pan. Add mushrooms, onions, and garlic and sauté over medium heat until onions are translucent. Add tomato sauce, basil, sugar, oregano, and pepper. Reduce heat and simmer uncovered about 30 minutes, stirring occasionally.

Spray a 9-inch square baking dish with nonstick cooking spray. Place half the lasagna noodles in a layer on the bottom; top with half the zucchini slices. Pour half the tomato sauce over zucchini. Combine the cottage cheese, Parmesan cheese, and flour. (For smoother texture, process cheese mixture in a blender or food processor until smooth.) Spread half of the cheese mixture over the layers in dish. Repeat with another layer of noodles, zucchini, tomato sauce mixture, and cheese mixture. Sprinkle mozzarella cheese over top of casserole. Bake, uncovered, at 350 degrees F. for 45 minutes. Remove from oven and let set 10 minutes before serving. Makes 6 servings.

NUTRITION (PER SERVING): 199 CALORIES

TOTAL FAT	8 g	(36% OF CALORIES)
PROTEIN	18 g	(37% OF CALORIES)
CARBOHYDRATES	14 g	(27% OF CALORIES)
CHOLESTEROL	23 mg	
SODIUM	962 mg	

Microwaved Baked Beans

½ cup green bell pepper strips
½ cup chopped onions
⅓ cup firmly packed brown sugar
1 teaspoon dry mustard
2 cans (16 ounces each) baked beans
1 can (20 ounces) pineapple tidbits in juice, drained

Arrange green pepper strips and onions on the bottom of a 12 x 8-inch microwavable baking dish. Cover and microwave on high setting for 3 minutes. In a medium mixing bowl, combine brown sugar and mustard. Stir in beans and pineapple and mix well. Stir in peppers and onions; return mixture to baking dish. Microwave, uncovered, on high setting for 8 to 10 minutes, stirring about halfway through cooking time. Makes 6 servings.

NUTRITION (PER SERVING): 274 CALORIES

TOTAL FAT	1 g	(3% OF CALORIES)
PROTEIN	8 g	(12% OF CALORIES)
CARBOHYDRATES	58 g	(85% OF CALORIES)
CHOLESTEROL	0 mg	
SODIUM	605 mg	

Baked Beans

58 ounces pork and beans in tomato sauce
2 cups chopped onions
2 cups chopped green bell peppers
1 cup ketchup
1 cup brown sugar
2 teaspoons Worcestershire sauce
1 pound Canadian bacon, cooked,
    cut in small pieces, and drained

Combine all ingredients well and pour into a 13 x 9-inch baking pan. Cover with aluminum foil and bake at 325 degrees F. for 2½ hours. Uncover and bake another 30 minutes. Makes 10 servings.

NUTRITION (PER SERVING): 365 CALORIES

TOTAL FAT	7 g	(16% OF CALORIES)
PROTEIN	20 g	(22% OF CALORIES)
CARBOHYDRATES	56 g	(61% OF CALORIES)
CHOLESTEROL	38 mg	
SODIUM	1674 mg	

Rice with Red Kidney Beans

1 tablespoon olive oil
1 cup chopped onions
1 cup chopped green bell peppers
3 cloves garlic, minced
2 cups chopped tomatoes
½ cup diced lean ham
1 can (15 ounces) red kidney beans, drained
2 cups cooked rice

Heat oil in a large frying pan. Add onions, green peppers, and garlic; sauté over medium heat until vegetables are tender. Add tomatoes and cook for about 2 minutes, stirring occasionally. Add ham, beans, and cooked rice to mixture, stir well, and cook for 2 minutes longer or until heated through. Makes 6 servings.

NUTRITION (PER SERVING): 220 CALORIES

TOTAL FAT	4 g	(15% OF CALORIES)
PROTEIN	9 g	(15% OF CALORIES)
CARBOHYDRATES	38 g	(70% OF CALORIES)
CHOLESTEROL	5 mg	
SODIUM	387 mg	

Lemon Pilaf

1½ cups chicken broth
¾ cup sliced celery
½ cup chopped onions
¼ cup uncooked brown rice
¼ cup uncooked whole wheat
3 tablespoons dried parsley flakes
1 tablespoon butter or margarine, melted
1½ teaspoons grated fresh lemon peel

Bring chicken broth to a boil in a medium saucepan. Add celery, onions, rice, and wheat. Reduce heat, cover, and simmer 45 to 50 minutes or until grains are tender and liquid is mostly absorbed. Add parsley flakes, melted butter or margarine, and lemon peel; stir to blend. Makes 4 servings.

NUTRITION (PER SERVING): 92 CALORIES

TOTAL FAT	4 g	(36% OF CALORIES)
PROTEIN	2 g	(9% OF CALORIES)
CARBOHYDRATES	13 g	(55% OF CALORIES)
CHOLESTEROL	0 mg	
SODIUM	606 mg	

Lemon Chive Couscous

¾ cup chicken broth
½ cup uncooked couscous
1 teaspoon grated fresh lemon peel
⅛ teaspoon turmeric
¼ cup chopped fresh chives
1 dash salt

Bring chicken broth to boil in a small saucepan. Remove from heat; stir in couscous, lemon peel, turmeric, chives, and salt. Cover and let stand 5 minutes. Fluff with a fork. Makes 4 servings.

NUTRITION (PER SERVING): 91 CALORIES

TOTAL FAT	LESS THAN 1 g	(4% OF CALORIES)
PROTEIN	3 g	(15% OF CALORIES)
CARBOHYDRATES	19 g	(82% OF CALORIES)
CHOLESTEROL	0 mg	
SODIUM	276 mg	

Spanish Rice

¼ cup butter or margarine
2 cups uncooked instant rice
1 can (14½ ounces) chopped stewed
   tomatoes, undrained
1 cup hot water
1 cup chopped onions
2 teaspoons beef bouillon granules
1 clove garlic, minced
1 teaspoon sugar
1 teaspoon salt
¼ teaspoon pepper

Melt butter in a saucepan over medium heat. Stir in uncooked rice and sauté until browned. Add tomatoes with liquid, water, onions, bouillon, garlic, sugar, salt, and pepper; stir to mix thoroughly. Bring to a boil. Reduce heat and simmer, covered, until the liquid is absorbed and rice is tender, about 10 to 15 minutes. Makes 6 servings.

NUTRITION (PER SERVING): 333 CALORIES

TOTAL FAT	8 g	(23% OF CALORIES)
PROTEIN	6 g	(7% OF CALORIES)
CARBOHYDRATES	59 g	(71% OF CALORIES)
CHOLESTEROL	21 mg	
SODIUM	871 mg	

Wild Rice Pilaf

Pictured on page 63.

2 tablespoons butter
1 cup uncooked long-grain wild rice
¼ cup finely chopped onions
⅓ cup finely chopped celery
3 cups hot chicken broth
2 tablespoons chopped parsley
¼ cup slivered almonds

Melt butter in frying pan over medium heat. Add rice, onions, and celery; stir and cook until slightly brown. Add chicken broth. Reduce heat to low; cover and simmer until moisture has been absorbed and rice is tender, about 15 to 20 minutes. Just before serving, add parsley and almonds and toss lightly. Makes 8 servings.

NUTRITION (PER SERVING): 91 CALORIES

TOTAL FAT	6 g	(62% OF CALORIES)
PROTEIN	2 g	(9% OF CALORIES)
CARBOHYDRATES	7 g	(29% OF CALORIES)
CHOLESTEROL	8 mg	
SODIUM	682 mg	

Rice with Herbs

2 tablespoons butter or margarine
1 cup uncooked long-grain rice
4 green onions, cut into 1-inch pieces
½ teaspoon tarragon
½ teaspoon thyme
½ teaspoon basil
½ teaspoon dried parsley flakes
½ teaspoon pepper
2 cups chicken broth
Salt to taste

Melt butter or margarine in a medium saucepan.
Add rice and green onions; sauté over medium-high
heat for 2 to 3 minutes or until onion is tender. Add
tarragon, thyme, basil, parsley flakes, and pepper;
cook 1 minute more. Stir in broth and salt and
bring to a boil. Reduce heat to low; cover and
simmer until liquid is absorbed and rice is tender,
about 15 minutes. Makes 6 servings.

NUTRITION (PER SERVING):   164 CALORIES

TOTAL FAT	4 g	(21% OF CALORIES)
PROTEIN	1 g	(3% OF CALORIES)
CARBOHYDRATES	31 g	(76% OF CALORIES)
CHOLESTEROL	31 mg	
SODIUM	851 mg	

Homemade Flavored-Rice Mix

3 cups uncooked long-grain rice
6 teaspoons chicken bouillon granules
¼ cup dried parsley flakes
2 teaspoons onion powder
½ teaspoon garlic powder
¼ teaspoon thyme

Mix all ingredients together and store in a container
with a tight-fitting lid. To prepare, bring 2 cups of
water to a boil in a medium saucepan. Add 1
tablespoon butter or margarine and 1 cup rice mix.
Reduce heat and simmer, covered, until liquid is
absorbed and rice is tender, about 15 minutes.
Makes 6 servings. (Mix makes enough for about 3
batches as prepared according to instructions.)

NUTRITION (PER SERVING AS PREPARED):   146 CALORIES

TOTAL FAT	2 g	(12% OF CALORIES)
PROTEIN	1 g	(3% OF CALORIES)
CARBOHYDRATES	31 g	(85% OF CALORIES)
CHOLESTEROL	1 mg	
SODIUM	755 mg	

SALADS AND SALAD DRESSINGS

Apple Valley Slaw

½ head green cabbage, shredded
2 medium Red Delicious apples, unpeeled and diced
½ cup chopped green onions
1 green bell pepper, slivered
½ teaspoon sugar
½ teaspoon seasoned salt
¼ teaspoon pepper
1 cup light mayonnaise
¼ cup sugar
⅓ cup vinegar

Toss cabbage, apples, green onions, and green peppers together in large bowl. Sprinkle with ½ teaspoon sugar, seasoned salt, and pepper. Combine mayonnaise, ¼ cup sugar, and vinegar. Pour over cabbage mixture and toss lightly. Makes 12 servings.

NUTRITION (PER SERVING): 103 CALORIES

TOTAL FAT	4 g	(36% OF CALORIES)
PROTEIN	1 g	(3% OF CALORIES)
CARBOHYDRATES	16 g	(62% OF CALORIES)
CHOLESTEROL	5 mg	
SODIUM	283 mg	

Coleslaw

½ cup light mayonnaise
⅓ cup nonfat sour cream
2 tablespoons sugar
½ teaspoon lemon juice
1½ tablespoons white vinegar
3 cups chopped or shredded cabbage
1 medium carrot, shredded
1 can (8 ounces) pineapple tidbits in juice, drained
½ cup raisins

In a small bowl, combine mayonnaise, sour cream, sugar, lemon juice, and vinegar to make dressing. Set aside. In large bowl, combine cabbage, carrot, pineapple, and raisins. Pour dressing over cabbage mixture and mix thoroughly. Chill at least 30 minutes before serving. Makes 6 servings.

NUTRITION (PER SERVING): 148 CALORIES

TOTAL FAT	4 g	(24% OF CALORIES)
PROTEIN	2 g	(5% OF CALORIES)
CARBOHYDRATES	26 g	(71% OF CALORIES)
CHOLESTEROL	14 mg	
SODIUM	120 mg	

Cabbage Tuna Toss

⅓ cup light mayonnaise
⅓ cup nonfat plain yogurt
2 teaspoons prepared mustard
¾ teaspoon dill
3 cups shredded cabbage
1 can (6½ ounces) chunk light tuna in water,
   drained and broken into chunks
¾ cup sliced fresh mushrooms
1 tomato, cut into thin wedges
½ cucumber, thinly sliced
12 pitted black olives, halved lengthwise
6 radishes, thinly sliced

In a small bowl, stir together mayonnaise, yogurt, mustard, and dill. Cover; chill for several hours to blend flavors. In a large salad bowl, combine shredded cabbage, tuna, mushrooms, tomato wedges, cucumbers, olives, and radishes. (This can also be done several hours ahead of time, if desired; cover tightly and refrigerate.) Just before serving, pour dressing over salad; toss lightly to mix. Makes 4 servings.

NUTRITION (PER SERVING): 136 CALORIES

TOTAL FAT	4 g	(26% OF CALORIES)
PROTEIN	15 g	(44% OF CALORIES)
CARBOHYDRATES	10 g	(30% OF CALORIES)
CHOLESTEROL	25 mg	
SODIUM	427 mg	

Festive Potato Salad

Pictured on page 89.

¼ cup olive oil or vegetable oil
¼ cup red wine vinegar
1 tablespoon sugar
1½ teaspoons chili powder
1 dash bottled hot pepper sauce
2 pounds red potatoes, peeled, cooked, and cubed
1½ cups whole kernel corn
1 cup shredded carrots
½ cup chopped red onions
½ cup diced green bell peppers
½ cup diced red bell peppers
½ cup sliced ripe olives (optional)
Salt and pepper to taste

Combine olive oil, vinegar, sugar, chili powder, and hot pepper sauce. Cover and refrigerate at least 30 minutes to blend flavors. In a large salad bowl, mix potato cubes, corn, carrots, onions, green and red peppers, and olives. Pour chilled dressing over vegetables and toss gently to coat. Cover and chill to blend flavors. Just before serving, sprinkle with salt and pepper to taste. Makes 14 servings.

NUTRITION (PER SERVING): 101 CALORIES

TOTAL FAT	5 g	(44% OF CALORIES)
PROTEIN	2 g	(5% OF CALORIES)
CARBOHYDRATES	21 g	(51% OF CALORIES)
CHOLESTEROL	0 mg	
SODIUM	11 mg	

Southwestern Pasta Salad

½ cup tomato juice

¼ cup lime juice

¼ cup vegetable oil

½ teaspoon salt

¼ teaspoon pepper

2 cloves garlic, crushed

1 package (16 ounces) bowtie or farfalle pasta

2 cups tomatoes, seeded and coarsely chopped

1½ cups coarsely chopped cucumbers

½ cup diced red bell peppers

½ cup diced yellow bell peppers

⅓ cup sliced green onions

1 Anaheim chili pepper, seeded and chopped

1 small can (2¼ ounces) sliced ripe olives, drained

½ cup finely chopped fresh cilantro

Mix together the tomato juice, lime juice, oil, salt, pepper, and garlic. Cover and chill to blend flavors.

Cook pasta as directed on package. Drain and rinse under cold running water. In a large salad bowl, combine tomatoes, cucumbers, red and yellow peppers, green onions, chili pepper, olives, and cilantro. Add the pasta and toss gently. Pour chilled dressing over salad. Makes 14 servings.

NUTRITION (PER SERVING): 55 CALORIES

TOTAL FAT	4 g	(70% OF CALORIES)
PROTEIN	1 g	(5% OF CALORIES)
CARBOHYDRATES	3 g	(26% OF CALORIES)
CHOLESTEROL	0 mg	
SODIUM	162 mg	

Island Pasta Salad

1 package (8 ounces) spiral pasta

1 can (20 ounces) pineapple chunks in juice

1 small bottle (8 ounces) oil-free Italian dressing

¼ cup chopped cilantro or parsley

2 cups snow peas

1 cup sliced carrots

1 cup sliced cucumbers

Cook pasta according to package directions, omitting fat and salt. Drain and rinse under cold running water. Drain pineapple, reserving ¼ cup juice. Mix reserved juice with Italian dressing and cilantro or parsley. In a large salad bowl, combine pasta, pineapple, snow peas, carrots, and cucumbers. Pour dressing over and toss gently to mix. Makes 8 servings.

NUTRITION (PER SERVING): 184 CALORIES

TOTAL FAT	0 g	(0% OF CALORIES)
PROTEIN	5 g	(11% OF CALORIES)
CARBOHYDRATES	41 g	(89% OF CALORIES)
CHOLESTEROL	1 mg	
SODIUM	131 mg	

Tangy Tomato Slices

¼ cup vegetable oil

2 teaspoons vinegar

¼ cup fresh minced parsley

1 tablespoon basil

1 teaspoon sugar

1 teaspoon salt

½ teaspoon pepper

½ teaspoon dry mustard

½ teaspoon garlic powder

1 large sweet onion, thinly sliced

6 large tomatoes, thinly sliced

Combine oil, vinegar, parsley, basil, sugar, salt, pepper, mustard, and garlic powder; mix thoroughly. Layer onion and tomato slices in a shallow glass dish. Pour marinade over; cover and refrigerate for several hours. Makes 12 servings.

NUTRITION (PER SERVING): 70 CALORIES

TOTAL FAT	5 g	(63% OF CALORIES)
PROTEIN	1 g	(5% OF CALORIES)
CARBOHYDRATES	6 g	(32% OF CALORIES)
CHOLESTEROL	0 mg	
SODIUM	203 mg	

Tortellini Primavera Salad

1 package (8 ounces) tortellini

2 cups broccoli florets

2 cups sliced carrots

½ cup chopped green onions

½ cup chopped red bell peppers

½ cup chopped green bell peppers

½ cup light mayonnaise

1 teaspoon grated orange peel (optional)

1 teaspoon basil

½ teaspoon thyme

½ teaspoon salt

¼ teaspoon black pepper

8 lettuce leaves

¼ cup shredded part-skim mozzarella cheese

Cook tortellini in boiling water about 15 minutes or until tender. Drain and cool under cold running water. Steam broccoli florets and sliced carrots until tender–crisp. Cool under cold running water. Combine tortellini, broccoli, carrots, green onions, and red and green peppers. Mix mayonnaise, orange peel (if desired), basil, thyme, salt, and pepper. Pour over tortellini mixture. Toss to coat.

For each serving, line a salad plate with lettuce. Spoon on salad mixture and sprinkle lightly with shredded cheese. Serve chilled or at room temperature. Makes 8 servings.

NUTRITION (PER SERVING): 171 CALORIES

TOTAL FAT	6 g	(30% OF CALORIES)
PROTEIN	7 g	(17% OF CALORIES)
CARBOHYDRATES	23 g	(53% OF CALORIES)
CHOLESTEROL	19 mg	
SODIUM	366 mg	

Cucumber Salad

1 cup light sour cream
¼ cup chopped red onions
2 tablespoons lemon juice
2 tablespoons cider vinegar
1 tablespoon sugar
¼ teaspoon salt
⅛ teaspoon pepper
3 cucumbers, peeled and thinly sliced

Combine sour cream, onions, lemon juice, vinegar, sugar, salt, and pepper in a medium bowl. Stir in cucumber slices, mixing well. Cover and refrigerate for at least 1 hour to blend flavors. Makes 8 servings.

NUTRITION (PER SERVING): 56 CALORIES

TOTAL FAT	2 g	(34% OF CALORIES)
PROTEIN	2 g	(17% OF CALORIES)
CARBOHYDRATES	7 g	(49% OF CALORIES)
CHOLESTEROL	5 mg	
SODIUM	135 mg	

Corn Salad

2 cups fresh or frozen whole kernel corn
¾ cup chopped tomatoes
½ cup chopped green bell peppers
½ cup chopped celery
¼ cup chopped onions
¼ cup light ranch-style dressing

Combine corn, tomatoes, green peppers, celery, and onions in a large salad bowl. Pour dressing over and toss gently to coat. Cover and refrigerate at least 30 minutes to blend flavors. Makes 8 servings.

NUTRITION (PER SERVING): 87 CALORIES

TOTAL FAT	3 g	(31% OF CALORIES)
PROTEIN	2 g	(10% OF CALORIES)
CARBOHYDRATES	13 g	(59% OF CALORIES)
CHOLESTEROL	0 mg	
SODIUM	80 mg	

Crunchy Vegetable Salad

Pictured on cover.

2 cups cauliflower florets
2 cups broccoli florets
2 carrots, thinly sliced
1 small zucchini, sliced
1 small red onion, sliced
1 small bottle (8 ounces) oil-free Italian dressing

In a large bowl, combine cauliflower, broccoli, carrots, zucchini, and onions. Pour Italian dressing over vegetables and toss to coat evenly. Refrigerate at least 30 minutes to blend flavors. Makes 6 servings.

NUTRITION (PER SERVING): 72 CALORIES

TOTAL FAT	0 g	(0% OF CALORIES)
PROTEIN	3 g	(17% OF CALORIES)
CARBOHYDRATES	15 g	(83% OF CALORIES)
CHOLESTEROL	0 mg	
SODIUM	390 mg	

Marinated Mushroom Salad

2 quarts water
3 tablespoons lemon juice
3 pounds small fresh mushrooms
½ cup oil-free Italian dressing
½ cup red wine vinegar
½ teaspoon oregano
½ teaspoon salt
1 garlic clove, minced
1 cup sliced carrots
1 cup sliced celery
½ cup chopped green bell peppers
½ cup chopped onions
1 tablespoon minced fresh parsley
½ cup sliced pimiento-stuffed green olives
1 small can (2¼ ounces) sliced ripe olives, drained

Heat water to boiling in a large saucepan. Add lemon juice and mushrooms; boil for 3 minutes, stirring occasionally. Drain mushrooms and set aside to cool. Meanwhile, combine Italian dressing, vinegar, oregano, salt, and garlic; mix well. In a large salad bowl, toss together the cooled mushrooms, carrots, celery, green peppers, onions, parsley, and olives. Pour dressing over and stir to coat vegetables. Cover and marinate several hours or overnight in refrigerator. Makes 8 servings.

NUTRITION (PER SERVING): 107 CALORIES

TOTAL FAT	3 g	(25% OF CALORIES)
PROTEIN	4 g	(16% OF CALORIES)
CARBOHYDRATES	16 g	(60% OF CALORIES)
CHOLESTEROL	0 mg	
SODIUM	417 mg	

Strawberry Fruit Salad

1 medium red apple
1 cup halved seedless green grapes
1 cup sliced strawberries
½ cup sliced celery
¼ cup raisins
½ cup low-fat lemon, peach, or strawberry yogurt
2 tablespoons sunflower seeds, toasted

Core and chop unpeeled apple and place in a medium bowl. Add grapes, strawberries, celery, and raisins and mix gently. Fold in yogurt. Cover and refrigerate at least 30 minutes to blend flavors. When ready to serve, mix in sunflower seeds. Makes 6 servings.

NUTRITION (PER SERVING): 103 CALORIES

TOTAL FAT	2 g	(19% OF CALORIES)
PROTEIN	2 g	(8% OF CALORIES)
CARBOHYDRATES	19 g	(74% OF CALORIES)
CHOLESTEROL	1 mg	
SODIUM	21 mg	

Quick Fruit Salad

Pictured on page 63.

3 firm ripe bananas, sliced
2 cups strawberries, halved
1 cup seedless grapes
1 can (21 ounces) cherry or peach pie filling

Combine bananas, strawberries, and grapes in a medium bowl. Stir in pie filling, mixing well to coat. Refrigerate until ready to serve. Makes 8 servings.

NUTRITION (PER SERVING): 155 CALORIES

TOTAL FAT	1 g	(5% OF CALORIES)
PROTEIN	1 g	(5% OF CALORIES)
CARBOHYDRATES	36 g	(94% OF CALORIES)
CHOLESTEROL	0 mg	
SODIUM	8 mg	

Trifle Fruit Salad

2 cups fresh pineapple chunks
1 pint fresh strawberries, sliced
1 pint blueberries
2 cups seedless green grapes
1¼ cups skim milk
½ cup light sour cream
1 package instant banana cream pudding mix
1 small can (8 ounces) crushed pineapple, undrained

In a large glass serving bowl, layer fresh pineapple, strawberries, blueberries, and grapes. In a separate bowl, blend milk and sour cream; add pudding mix and beat for 2 minutes or until well blended. Stir in crushed pineapple. Spoon mixture over fruits in bowl to within 1 inch of edge. Cover and refrigerate several hours to blend flavors. Garnish with fresh fruits as desired. Makes 12 servings.

NUTRITION (PER SERVING): 120 CALORIES

TOTAL FAT	2 g	(16% OF CALORIES)
PROTEIN	2 g	(8% OF CALORIES)
CARBOHYDRATES	23 g	(77% OF CALORIES)
CHOLESTEROL	5 mg	
SODIUM	59 mg	

Raspberry Gelatin Salad

1¼ cups boiling water
1 package (3 ounces) strawberry-
    or raspberry-flavored gelatin
1 package (10 ounces) frozen raspberries
    (about 1⅓ cups), not thawed
1 small can (8 ounces) crushed
    pineapple in juice, undrained
½ cup sliced bananas
½ cup chopped pecans
Lettuce leaves
1 cup nonfat sour cream

Pour boiling water over gelatin. Stir for 2 minutes to dissolve thoroughly. Add raspberries, pineapple with juice, bananas, and pecans. Pour into individual molds and chill until firm. Unmold onto lettuce leaves and top with sour cream. Makes 10 servings.

NUTRITION (PER SERVING): 150 CALORIES

TOTAL FAT	4 g	(24% OF CALORIES)
PROTEIN	3 g	(9% OF CALORIES)
CARBOHYDRATES	25 g	(67% OF CALORIES)
CHOLESTEROL	0 mg	
SODIUM	45 mg	

Cran-Cherry Salad

2 packages (3 ounces each) cherry-flavored gelatin
1 cup sugar
2 cups boiling water
1 can (20 ounces) crushed pineapple
    in juice, undrained
3 cups fresh or frozen cranberries, chopped
1½ cups diced apples
1 cup chopped celery
½ cup chopped walnuts

Combine gelatin and sugar in a large bowl and pour boiling water over; stir to dissolve. Add pineapple with juice, cranberries, apples, celery, and walnuts and stir well. Pour into a 2-quart mold. Refrigerate 3 to 4 hours or until firm. Makes 16 servings.

NUTRITION (PER SERVING): 159 CALORIES

TOTAL FAT	2 g	(12% OF CALORIES)
PROTEIN	2 g	(5% OF CALORIES)
CARBOHYDRATES	33 g	(83% OF CALORIES)
CHOLESTEROL	0 mg	
SODIUM	42 mg	

Fresh Fruit Mold

1 fresh grapefruit
1 envelope (1 tablespoon) unflavored gelatin
½ cup sugar
¼ teaspoon salt
¼ cup water
¼ cup fresh lemon juice
1 cup orange juice (fresh or
*   reconstituted from frozen)*
½ cup seedless red grapes, halved
½ cup thinly sliced bananas

Peel and section grapefruit. Cut sections in thirds. Place in bowl to allow juices to accumulate.

Meanwhile, combine gelatin, sugar, and salt in a small saucepan. Stir in water and lemon juice. Cook, stirring constantly, over medium heat until gelatin is dissolved, 3 to 4 minutes. Remove from heat. Drain grapefruit sections, squeezing juice from membrane into bowl before discarding. Measure juice; add water if necessary to make ¼ cup. Add to gelatin mixture, along with orange juice. Chill until slightly thickened.

Fold grapes and bananas into gelatin. Pour into a 3-cup mold. Chill at least 2 hours or until firm. Makes 6 servings.

NUTRITION (PER SERVING):   159 CALORIES

TOTAL FAT	LESS THAN 1 g	(2% OF CALORIES)
PROTEIN	4 g	(10% OF CALORIES)
CARBOHYDRATES	35 g	(88% OF CALORIES)
CHOLESTEROL	0 mg	
SODIUM	97 mg	

Tropical Fruit Salad

½ cup nonfat plain yogurt
2 tablespoons orange marmalade
*   or apricot preserves*
¼ teaspoon poppy seeds
1 small fresh pineapple, peeled and sliced
1 mango or papaya, peeled and sliced
1 medium banana, sliced
1 kiwi fruit, peeled and sliced
2 tablespoons toasted coconut

Combine yogurt, marmalade or preserves, and poppy seeds in a small bowl. Mix well. On a serving platter, arrange pineapple, mango or papaya, banana, and kiwi in a decorative pattern. Sprinkle with coconut. Drizzle yogurt mixture over salad. Makes 6 servings.

Note: To toast coconut, spread on cookie sheet; bake at 350 degrees F. for 7 to 8 minutes or until light golden brown, stirring occasionally.

NUTRITION (PER SERVING):   256 CALORIES

TOTAL FAT	3 g	(10% OF CALORIES)
PROTEIN	2 g	(4% OF CALORIES)
CARBOHYDRATES	55 g	(86% OF CALORIES)
CHOLESTEROL	2 mg	
SODIUM	15 mg	

Strawberry Dressing for Fruit Salad

1 package (10 ounces) frozen strawberries,
   thawed and drained
⅔ cup nonfat mayonnaise
1 container (8 ounces) low-fat strawberry yogurt
Mint leaves

Combine strawberries and mayonnaise, then fold in yogurt. Cover and chill for 1 hour. Serve over fresh fruit (cantaloupe, honeydew, strawberries). Garnish with mint leaves. Makes 12 servings, about ¼ cup each.

NUTRITION (PER SERVING):   38 CALORIES

TOTAL FAT	0 g	(6% OF CALORIES)
PROTEIN	1 g	(9% OF CALORIES)
CARBOHYDRATES	8 g	(85% OF CALORIES)
CHOLESTEROL	1 mg	
SODIUM	168 mg	

Lion House French Dressing

1 cup sugar
1 cup ketchup
1 cup vinegar
1 cup apple juice
1 teaspoon dry mustard
¼ teaspoon pepper
½ cup chopped onions
1½ teaspoons lemon juice
½ teaspoon Worcestershire sauce

Combine all ingredients and mix well. Store in refrigerator. Makes 24 servings, about 2 tablespoons each.

NUTRITION (PER SERVING):   54 CALORIES

TOTAL FAT	LESS THAN 1 g	(2% OF CALORIES)
PROTEIN	LESS THAN 1 g	(2% OF CALORIES)
CARBOHYDRATES	13 g	(96% OF CALORIES)
CHOLESTEROL	0 mg	
SODIUM	119 mg	

Buttermilk Dressing

¾ cup nonfat buttermilk
2 tablespoons chopped green onions
1 tablespoon chopped fresh parsley
2 tablespoons 1% low-fat cottage cheese
¼ teaspoon dry mustard
1 drop Tabasco sauce

Mix all ingredients together in a blender until smooth. Serve over tossed greens. Makes 8 servings, about 2 tablespoons each.

NUTRITION (PER SERVING):   13 CALORIES

TOTAL FAT	LESS THAN 1 g	(18% OF CALORIES)
PROTEIN	1 g	(39% OF CALORIES)
CARBOHYDRATES	2 g	(43% OF CALORIES)
CHOLESTEROL	1 mg	
SODIUM	39 mg	

Ginger Chews (page 128), Brownies (page 132), Date Bars with Orange Icing (page 135), Seafood Shells (page 4), Salsa (page 5) with tortilla chips

VEGETABLES

Creamed Peas and Red Potatoes

4 medium red potatoes
1 package (10 ounces) frozen green peas
1 teaspoon sugar
2 tablespoons butter or margarine
2 tablespoons flour
½ teaspoon salt
¼ teaspoon white pepper
1½ cups 1% low-fat milk
2 tablespoons minced fresh dill weed

Cut unpeeled potatoes into 1½-inch cubes. Place cubes in a medium saucepan and add enough water just to cover them. Bring to a boil; reduce heat and cook, uncovered, until potatoes are tender, about 15 to 20 minutes. Prepare peas according to instructions on package, adding the sugar to the water used for cooking. Melt butter or margarine in a saucepan over medium heat. Stir in flour, salt, and pepper until smooth. Add milk gradually, stirring constantly, and continue cooking and stirring until mixture thickens and bubbles. Add dill. Drain potatoes and peas; pour sauce over them and stir to combine thoroughly. Serve immediately. Makes 8 servings.

NUTRITION (PER SERVING): 191 CALORIES

TOTAL FAT	4 g	(17% OF CALORIES)
PROTEIN	6 g	(13% OF CALORIES)
CARBOHYDRATES	34 g	(70% OF CALORIES)
CHOLESTEROL	10 mg	
SODIUM	247 mg	

Potato Casserole

5 large potatoes
1 can (10½ ounces) reduced-fat
    cream of chicken soup, undiluted
1 cup nonfat sour cream
1 cup 1% low-fat milk
3 tablespoons finely chopped green onions
½ cup grated sharp cheddar cheese
¾ cup bread crumbs or cornflake crumbs
2 tablespoons butter-flavored granules
3 tablespoons grated Parmesan cheese

Boil unpared potatoes until tender. Drain and peel. Shred coarsely. Place in 13 x 9-inch baking dish. Mix together soup, nonfat sour cream, milk, onions, and cheese. Pour evenly over potatoes. Do not mix. Mix crumbs with butter-flavored granules and Parmesan cheese; sprinkle over casserole. Bake, uncovered, for 30 minutes at 325 degrees F. Makes 10 servings.

NUTRITION (PER SERVING): 167 CALORIES

TOTAL FAT	5 g	(27% OF CALORIES)
PROTEIN	8 g	(18% OF CALORIES)
CARBOHYDRATES	23 g	(55% OF CALORIES)
CHOLESTEROL	11 mg	
SODIUM	422 mg	

Red Potato Medley

2 tablespoons butter or margarine
3 cups (about 2½ pounds) cubed red potatoes
1½ cups sliced carrots
¾ cup chopped onions
¼ cup minced fresh parsley
1 clove garlic, minced
¼ teaspoon salt
¼ teaspoon pepper

Melt butter or margarine in a large frying pan over medium heat. Stir in potatoes, carrots, onions, parsley, garlic, salt, and pepper; mix well. Reduce heat and cook, covered, for 15 to 20 minutes or until vegetables are tender, stirring occasionally. Makes 6 servings.

NUTRITION (PER SERVING): 129 CALORIES

TOTAL FAT	4 g	(28% OF CALORIES)
PROTEIN	2 g	(7% OF CALORIES)
CARBOHYDRATES	21 g	(65% OF CALORIES)
CHOLESTEROL	10 mg	
SODIUM	154 mg	

Cheese-Stuffed Potatoes

6 large potatoes
½ cup shredded reduced-fat cheddar cheese
½ cup shredded part-skim mozzarella cheese
⅓ cup chopped onions
½ cup fat-free ranch-style dressing

Bake potatoes at 400 degrees F. for 60 to 70 minutes or until tender. Slice off about the top ½ inch of each potato and carefully scoop out the insides of the potato into a large mixing bowl. Add cheeses (reserving a little of each to sprinkle over tops), onions, and dressing; blend ingredients well with an electric mixer. Mound mixture into potato shells and sprinkle with reserved cheese. Return to oven for 10 minutes or until heated through. If desired, broil for the last minute of cooking time to brown cheese slightly. Makes 6 servings.

NUTRITION (PER SERVING): 238 CALORIES

TOTAL FAT	3 g	(30% OF CALORIES)
PROTEIN	14 g	(24% OF CALORIES)
CARBOHYDRATES	38 g	(64% OF CALORIES)
CHOLESTEROL	11 mg	
SODIUM	300 mg	

New Potatoes Dijon

¼ cup tarragon vinegar (white
   vinegar may be substituted)
3 tablespoons vegetable oil
1 tablespoon Dijon mustard
¼ teaspoon salt
¼ teaspoon basil
⅛ teaspoon pepper
1 pound small new potatoes
1 cup torn fresh spinach

Combine vinegar, oil, mustard, salt, basil, and pepper; blend thoroughly. Cover and place in refrigerator.

Scrub potatoes and peel a narrow strip of skin from around the center of each. Place in a medium saucepan and add water to cover. Bring to a boil; cover and cook 10 to 15 minutes or until potatoes are tender. Drain well and pour chilled dressing over potatoes, tossing to coat. Cover and let stand in refrigerator several hours or overnight, stirring occasionally. When ready to serve, add spinach and toss lightly. Makes 6 servings.

NUTRITION (PER SERVING): 150 CALORIES

TOTAL FAT	7 g	(43% OF CALORIES)
PROTEIN	2 g	(6% OF CALORIES)
CARBOHYDRATES	19 g	(51% OF CALORIES)
CHOLESTEROL	0 mg	
SODIUM	174 mg	

Tater Puffs

1 tablespoon light margarine
⅓ cup finely chopped onions
½ cup cooked mashed potatoes
1 cup cooked brown rice
1 tablespoon tomato paste
½ teaspoon salt
½ cup whole-grain bread crumbs
3 tablespoons grated Parmesan cheese
1 dash Tabasco sauce

In a medium saucepan, melt margarine over medium heat. Add onions and cook, stirring frequently, until translucent. Remove from heat and stir in mashed potatoes, rice, tomato paste, salt, bread crumbs, cheese, and Tabasco sauce. Mix well. Form into 1½-inch balls; place on a baking sheet sprayed with nonstick cooking spray. Bake at 350 degrees F. for 15 to 20 minutes or until lightly browned. Makes 4 servings.

NUTRITION (PER SERVING): 163 CALORIES

TOTAL FAT	3 g	(17% OF CALORIES)
PROTEIN	6 g	(15% OF CALORIES)
CARBOHYDRATES	28 g	(68% OF CALORIES)
CHOLESTEROL	4 mg	
SODIUM	576 mg	

Potato Cheese Pie

5 potatoes (about 1¼ pounds), peeled and halved
1½ cups 1% low-fat cottage cheese
1 large egg
¼ teaspoon black pepper
2 tablespoons chopped green onions
1 cup shredded reduced-fat cheddar cheese

Place the potatoes in a medium saucepan and add enough water to cover. Bring to a boil; cover and cook until tender, 20 to 25 minutes. Drain well.

While potatoes are cooking, combine cottage cheese, egg, and pepper in the container of a blender or food processor. Blend for 8 to 10 seconds to mix well.

Spray a 9-inch square baking dish with nonstick cooking spray. Slice potatoes in ¼-inch slices and layer ⅓ of them on the bottom of the dish. Spread ½ of the cottage cheese mixture evenly over the potato slices. Sprinkle with ⅓ of the green onions and cheddar cheese. Layer another ⅓ of the potatoes and the remaining cottage cheese mixture, then top with remaining ⅓ of potatoes and the rest of the green onions and cheddar cheese. Bake, uncovered, at 375 degrees F. for 35 to 40 minutes or until cheese is golden brown. Makes 4 servings.

NUTRITION (PER SERVING): 222 CALORIES

TOTAL FAT	6 g	(24% OF CALORIES)
PROTEIN	20 g	(36% OF CALORIES)
CARBOHYDRATES	22 g	(40% OF CALORIES)
CHOLESTEROL	87 mg	
SODIUM	557 mg	

Broccoli and Mushroom Stuffed Potatoes

4 large potatoes
1 cup 1% low-fat cottage cheese
3 tablespoons skim milk
⅛ teaspoon pepper
1 cup chopped fresh broccoli
1 cup sliced mushrooms
¼ cup minced fresh chives

Bake potatoes at 400 degrees F. for 60 to 70 minutes or until tender. Slice off about the top ½ inch of each potato and carefully scoop out the insides of the potato into a large mixing bowl. Add cottage cheese, milk, and pepper, and mash to desired consistency with a potato masher. Spray a frying pan with nonstick cooking spray; add broccoli and mushrooms and sauté until tender. Add to potato mixture along with chives, mixing well to blend. Fill the potato shells with mixture. Bake for 30 minutes at 350 degrees F. Makes 4 servings.

Note: Potatoes can be stuffed ahead of time, wrapped, and refrigerated for several hours, if desired. Bring to room temperature before baking.

NUTRITION (PER SERVING): 186 CALORIES

TOTAL FAT	1 g	(6% OF CALORIES)
PROTEIN	11 g	(25% OF CALORIES)
CARBOHYDRATES	32 g	(69% OF CALORIES)
CHOLESTEROL	3 mg	
SODIUM	255 mg	

Quick and Easy Carrots

Pictured on page 63.

2 cups sliced carrots
1 tablespoon light butter or margarine
2 tablespoons sliced green onions
1 tablespoon water
¼ teaspoon salt
Chopped fresh parsley

Combine carrots, butter or margarine, green onions, water, and salt in a medium saucepan. Cover and simmer, stirring occasionally, for 8 to 10 minutes or until carrots are tender-crisp. Sprinkle with parsley. Makes 4 servings.

NUTRITION (PER SERVING): 46 CALORIES

TOTAL FAT	2 g	(40% OF CALORIES)
PROTEIN	1 g	(9% OF CALORIES)
CARBOHYDRATES	6 g	(51% OF CALORIES)
CHOLESTEROL	8 mg	
SODIUM	196 mg	

Dilly Carrots

3 cups sliced carrots
2 tablespoons water
¼ cup diced green bell peppers
2 tablespoons minced fresh dill weed
1 tablespoon honey
1 tablespoon light butter or margarine
2 teaspoons lemon juice
½ teaspoon salt
¼ teaspoon ginger

Place carrots with water in a medium saucepan. Cover and cook over medium-low heat until carrots are tender-crisp. Drain. Add green peppers, dill, honey, butter or margarine, lemon juice, salt, and ginger. Cook over low heat for 1 to 2 minutes longer, or until hot. Makes 4 servings.

NUTRITION (PER SERVING): 68 CALORIES

TOTAL FAT	2 g	(36% OF CALORIES)
PROTEIN	1 g	(5% OF CALORIES)
CARBOHYDRATES	11 g	(59% OF CALORIES)
CHOLESTEROL	8 mg	
SODIUM	352 mg	

Vegetable-Pasta-Cheese Bake

1 cup uncooked medium-size shell macaroni
1½ cups broccoli florets
1½ cups cauliflower florets
1 cup shredded carrots
1 cup sliced fresh mushrooms
1 cup shredded part-skim mozzarella cheese
1 teaspoon dried parsley flakes
½ teaspoon garlic powder
½ teaspoon marjoram
½ teaspoon oregano
½ teaspoon basil
¼ teaspoon salt

Cook macaroni according to instructions on package, leaving out any fat and salt. Drain well and set aside.

Steam broccoli, cauliflower, carrots, and mushrooms in a small amount of boiling water until tender-crisp, about 7 or 8 minutes. Combine cooked macaroni, steamed vegetables, cheese, parsley flakes, garlic powder, marjoram, oregano, basil, and salt; mix gently. Pour into a 2-quart casserole dish. Bake at 350 degrees F. for 10 minutes or until cheese melts. Makes 8 servings.

NUTRITION (PER SERVING): 115 CALORIES

TOTAL FAT	3 g	(22% OF CALORIES)
PROTEIN	7 g	(25% OF CALORIES)
CARBOHYDRATES	15 g	(53% OF CALORIES)
CHOLESTEROL	9 mg	
SODIUM	163 mg	

Sweet and Sour Cabbage

1 large head red cabbage, thinly sliced (about 7 cups)
½ cup chopped onions
¼ cup cider vinegar
2 tablespoons sugar
¼ teaspoon salt
⅛ teaspoon pepper
¾ cup coarsely shredded carrots
¼ cup raisins

In a 3-quart microwaveable baking dish, mix together the cabbage, onions, vinegar, sugar, salt, and pepper. Cover with plastic wrap or lid. Microwave on high setting for 10 to 12 minutes, stirring halfway through the cooking time. Add the carrots and raisins, stirring to mix well. Cover again and microwave on high setting for 5 to 6 minutes or until tender. Makes 4 servings.

NUTRITION (PER SERVING):   118 CALORIES

TOTAL FAT LESS THAN 1 g		(5% OF CALORIES)
PROTEIN	2 g	(9% OF CALORIES)
CARBOHYDRATES	26 g	(88% OF CALORIES)
CHOLESTEROL	0 mg	
SODIUM	170 mg	

Zucchini Frittata

1 medium zucchini
1 tablespoon olive oil
¼ cup finely chopped green onions
2 cloves garlic, minced
1 can (14½ ounces) chopped stewed tomatoes, drained
¼ teaspoon basil
¼ teaspoon thyme
⅛ teaspoon pepper
3 egg whites
1 whole egg
1 cup shredded part-skim mozzarella cheese

Cut the zucchini in half lengthwise, and slice the halves in ¼-inch-thick slices. Preheat the oil in a nonstick, ovenproof frying pan. Stir in green onions and cook over medium heat, stirring occasionally, for about 5 minutes or until tender. Add garlic, zucchini slices, tomatoes, basil, thyme, and pepper. Cover and cook about three minutes or until zucchini is tender.

Whisk together the egg whites and the whole egg. Add them to the vegetable mixture in the frying pan and sprinkle the cheese over the top. Preheat the oven to 350 degrees F. Place the frying pan on the middle rack and bake frittata, uncovered, about 5 minutes, until just set. Reset the oven to broil, and place frittata under the broiler 5 to 6 inches from the heat until golden, about 2 to 3 minutes. Serve immediately. Makes 4 servings.

NUTRITION (PER SERVING):   181 CALORIES

TOTAL FAT	10 g	(48% OF CALORIES)
PROTEIN	13 g	(29% OF CALORIES)
CARBOHYDRATES	10 g	(23% OF CALORIES)
CHOLESTEROL	70 mg	
SODIUM	268 mg	

Broccoli and Corn Casserole

1½ teaspoons flour
¼ teaspoon dry mustard
⅛ teaspoon salt
⅛ teaspoon pepper
½ cup 1% low-fat milk
½ cup chopped red onions
1 teaspoon vegetable oil
4 cups broccoli florets, coarsely chopped
    (about 1 large bunch)
1 package (10 ounces) frozen
    whole-kernel corn, thawed
¼ cup grated Parmesan cheese
1 tablespoon fine dry bread crumbs

Combine flour, mustard, salt, and pepper in a 2-cup glass measure. Gradually add milk, stirring well with a wire whisk. Microwave, uncovered, on high setting for 2 minutes, stirring halfway through. Set aside.

Combine onions and oil in an 8-inch square baking dish. Microwave, uncovered, on high setting for 1 minute. Stir in broccoli and corn. Cover with heavy-duty plastic wrap, cutting 2 or 3 small slits in wrap to vent. Microwave on high setting for 5 minutes, stirring halfway through. Add milk mixture and stir well. Cover and microwave on high setting for 2 to 3 minutes or until thoroughly heated. Stir in cheese and top with bread crumbs. Microwave on high setting, uncovered, for 1 minute. Let stand, uncovered, for 5 minutes. Makes 4 servings.

NUTRITION (PER SERVING): 161 CALORIES

TOTAL FAT	4 g	(21% OF CALORIES)
PROTEIN	8 g	(20% OF CALORIES)
CARBOHYDRATES	24 g	(59% OF CALORIES)
CHOLESTEROL	5 mg	
SODIUM	220 mg	

Garden Medley

3 or 4 ears fresh corn on the cob
¼ cup chopped onions
¼ cup chopped green bell peppers
2 tablespoons butter or margarine
½ teaspoon salt
¼ teaspoon cumin
1 large tomato, seeded and chopped
2 tablespoons sugar

Cut corn from cob and combine kernels in a medium saucepan with onions, green peppers, butter or margarine, salt, and cumin. Turn heat to medium and cook, stirring frequently, until butter melts. Reduce heat to low, cover pan, and cook for 10 minutes. Add tomatoes and sugar, stirring gently to blend. Cover and cook an additional 5 minutes. Makes 5 servings.

NUTRITION (PER SERVING): 154 CALORIES

TOTAL FAT	5 g	(30% OF CALORIES)
PROTEIN	3 g	(7% OF CALORIES)
CARBOHYDRATES	24 g	(63% OF CALORIES)
CHOLESTEROL	12 mg	
SODIUM	289 mg	

Oriental Spinach

1 pound fresh spinach
1 tablespoon olive oil
1 tablespoon soy sauce
½ teaspoon sugar
2 tablespoons finely chopped onions
1 can (8 ounces) water chestnuts, drained and sliced

Wash and pat spinach leaves dry. Tear into bite-size pieces. In large saucepan, simmer spinach with a small amount of water for 3 minutes; drain thoroughly. Heat olive oil, soy sauce, and sugar in skillet; add spinach and onions. Cook and toss until spinach is well coated, 2 to 3 minutes. Stir in water chestnuts. Makes 4 servings.

NUTRITION (PER SERVING): 100 CALORIES

TOTAL FAT	4 g	(34% OF CALORIES)
PROTEIN	4 g	(16% OF CALORIES)
CARBOHYDRATES	12 g	(49% OF CALORIES)
CHOLESTEROL	0 mg	
SODIUM	351 mg	

Vegetable Pan Pizza

2 tablespoons yellow or white cornmeal
1 package (1 scant tablespoon) active dry yeast
1 teaspoon sugar
1 cup warm water (110-115 degrees F.)
2¾ cups flour, divided
2 tablespoons vegetable oil
¼ teaspoon salt
1 can (8 ounces) pizza sauce
1 cup sliced fresh mushrooms
½ cup chopped green bell peppers
1 can (14 ounces) artichoke hearts, drained and chopped
¼ cup chopped onions
½ cup shredded part-skim mozzarella cheese
⅓ cup grated Parmesan cheese

Spray a 13 x 9-inch baking pan with nonstick cooking spray and sprinkle with cornmeal; set aside. In a large mixing bowl, combine yeast and sugar in warm water. Stir to dissolve. Let stand for 5 minutes. Add 2½ cups of the flour, oil, and salt. Stir until a soft dough forms. Sprinkle the remaining ¼ cup of flour on a flat surface and turn the dough out onto it. Working the flour into the dough, knead until dough is smooth and elastic–about 5 minutes. Shape into a ball and place in prepared pan. Let dough stand for 5 to 10 minutes to soften, then pat it evenly over bottom and up sides of pan. Spread the pizza sauce over the dough and arrange mushrooms, bell peppers, artichoke hearts, and onions on it. Sprinkle cheeses over top. Bake in lower third of oven at 425 degrees F. for 25 minutes. Makes 8 servings.

NUTRITION (PER SERVING): 278 CALORIES

TOTAL FAT	8 g	(25% OF CALORIES)
PROTEIN	9 g	(13% OF CALORIES)
CARBOHYDRATES	43 g	(62% OF CALORIES)
CHOLESTEROL	8 mg	
SODIUM	352 mg	

Grilled Marinated Vegetables

6 pattypan squash (about 2 inches in diameter)

3 zucchini or yellow summer squash, cut lengthwise in half

1 red or green bell pepper, cut into 6 pieces

1 large red onion, cut into ½-inch slices

3 tablespoons vegetable oil

1 tablespoon lemon juice

½ teaspoon marjoram

1 clove garlic, crushed

¼ teaspoon salt

⅛ teaspoon pepper

Arrange squash, peppers, and onions in a 13 x 9-inch baking dish. Mix oil, lemon juice, marjoram, and garlic together and pour over vegetables. Cover and marinate in refrigerator for at least 1 hour. Reserving marinade, remove vegetables and place on grill, 4 inches from coals. Grill for 10 to 15 minutes, turning and brushing 2 to 3 times with marinade. Cook until golden brown. Sprinkle with salt and pepper. Makes 6 servings.

NUTRITION (PER SERVING): 126 CALORIES

TOTAL FAT	7 g	(51% OF CALORIES)
PROTEIN	3 g	(10% OF CALORIES)
CARBOHYDRATES	12 g	(39% OF CALORIES)
CHOLESTEROL	0 mg	
SODIUM	103 mg	

Herbed Grilled Corn

½ cup light margarine, softened

2 tablespoons minced fresh parsley

2 tablespoons minced fresh chives

1 teaspoon thyme

½ teaspoon salt

¼ teaspoon cayenne pepper

8 ears sweet corn

In a small bowl, combine margarine, parsley, chives, thyme, salt, and cayenne pepper. Spread 1 tablespoon of mixture over each ear of corn. Wrap ears individually in heavy foil. Grill covered over medium coals, turning frequently, for 10 to 15 minutes or until corn is tender. Makes 8 servings.

NUTRITION (PER SERVING): 130 CALORIES

TOTAL FAT	6 g	(41% OF CALORIES)
PROTEIN	0 g	(0% OF CALORIES)
CARBOHYDRATES	19 g	(59% OF CALORIES)
CHOLESTEROL	0 mg	
SODIUM	286 mg	

French Peas

1 tablespoon light butter or margarine
½ cup water
½ cup fresh sliced mushrooms
1 package (10 ounces) frozen peas
1 small onion, thinly sliced
¼ teaspoon salt

In a medium saucepan, melt butter or margarine. Add water, mushrooms, peas, onion, and salt. Bring to a boil; reduce heat and simmer, covered, until the peas are tender, stirring occasionally. Makes 4 servings.

NUTRITION (PER SERVING): 106 CALORIES

TOTAL FAT	3 g	(28% OF CALORIES)
PROTEIN	5 g	(17% OF CALORIES)
CARBOHYDRATES	15 g	(55% OF CALORIES)
CHOLESTEROL	8 mg	
SODIUM	259 mg	

Sesame Green Beans

Pictured on cover.

2 cups (about 1 pound) fresh or frozen green beans
½ teaspoon salt
2 tablespoons light butter
1 tablespoon soy sauce
1 tablespoon toasted sesame seeds

Wash green beans. Snip ends and cut into ¼- to ½-inch lengths.* Cook in boiling salted water until just tender. Drain.

In a small saucepan, combine butter, soy sauce, and sesame seeds. Cook, stirring frequently, over medium heat until butter is melted and sauce is hot. Pour over cooked green beans. Makes 4 servings.

*Note: Beans may be left whole, if desired.

NUTRITION (PER SERVING): 60 CALORIES

TOTAL FAT	4 g	(65% OF CALORIES)
PROTEIN	2 g	(11% OF CALORIES)
CARBOHYDRATES	4 g	(24% OF CALORIES)
CHOLESTEROL	7 mg	
SODIUM	757 mg	

CAKES AND COOKIES

Chocolate Buttermilk Cake

Pictured on cover.

1⅔ cups flour
1 cup sugar
⅓ cup cocoa
1 teaspoon baking soda
½ teaspoon salt
1 cup nonfat buttermilk
¼ cup water
⅓ cup vegetable oil
1 teaspoon vanilla

Preheat oven to 375 degrees F. Coat a 9-inch round cake pan with nonstick cooking spray; set aside. In a large bowl, sift together flour, sugar, cocoa, baking soda, and salt. Make a well in center of mixture. Blend buttermilk, water, oil, and vanilla. Pour into well in dry ingredients, stirring until smooth. Pour into prepared cake pan and bake for 20 minutes or until a wooden toothpick inserted in center comes out clean. Cool completely in pan. Sprinkle lightly with confectioner's sugar, or top with Chocolate Glaze (page 127) or Fluffy Divinity Frosting (page 127). Makes 12 servings.

NUTRITION (PER SERVING): 198 CALORIES

TOTAL FAT	6 g	(30% OF CALORIES)
PROTEIN	3 g	(6% OF CALORIES)
CARBOHYDRATES	33 g	(64% OF CALORIES)
CHOLESTEROL	0 mg	
SODIUM	137 mg	

Sylvia's Fudge Cake

1¾ cups flour
1¾ cups sugar
¼ cup instant nonfat dry milk
¼ cup cocoa
2 teaspoons baking powder
¼ teaspoon baking soda
1 teaspoon salt
1½ cups water
1 teaspoon vanilla
3 egg whites
½ cup raspberry low-fat yogurt
½ teaspoon orange peel

Preheat oven to 350 degrees F. Spray a 13 x 9-inch pan with nonstick cooking spray; set aside.

Sift together the flour, sugar, dry milk, cocoa, baking powder, baking soda, and salt into a large bowl. Add water, vanilla, egg whites, yogurt, and orange peel. Mix until well blended. Bake for 30 to 35 minutes or until a wooden toothpick inserted in center comes out clean. Makes 12 servings.

NUTRITION (PER SERVING): 209 CALORIES

TOTAL FAT	1 g	(3% OF CALORIES)
PROTEIN	5 g	(9% OF CALORIES)
CARBOHYDRATES	46 g	(88% OF CALORIES)
CHOLESTEROL	1 mg	
SODIUM	301 mg	

Pineapple Sheet Cake

2 cups flour
1½ cups sugar
2 teaspoons baking soda
½ teaspoon salt
2 eggs
1 can (20 ounces) crushed pineapple
*   in juice, undrained*
1 teaspoon vanilla
1 cup chopped nuts

Preheat oven to 350 degrees F. Spray a 17 x 11-inch jelly roll pan with nonstick cooking spray. Combine flour, sugar, baking soda, and salt in a large bowl. Add eggs, pineapple with juice, and vanilla; mix until smooth. Add nuts. Bake for 35 minutes. Cool in pan. Makes 24 servings.

NUTRITION (PER SERVING): 142 CALORIES

TOTAL FAT	4 g	(23% OF CALORIES)
PROTEIN	3 g	(8% OF CALORIES)
CARBOHYDRATES	25 g	(70% OF CALORIES)
CHOLESTEROL	18 mg	
SODIUM	124 mg	

White Cake

5 tablespoons butter or margarine
¾ cup sugar
1 teaspoon vanilla
¼ teaspoon almond extract
1¾ cups sifted cake flour
2 teaspoons baking powder
⅛ teaspoon salt
⅔ cup milk
3 egg whites

Preheat oven to 375 degrees F. Spray a 9-inch springform pan with nonstick cooking spray; set aside.

In large mixer bowl, beat butter or margarine to soften. Reserve 2 tablespoons from the ¾ cup sugar; gradually add the rest to the butter, continuing to beat until light. Mix in vanilla and almond extracts.

Sift together the flour, baking powder, and salt. Add dry ingredients to creamed mixture alternately with the milk, beating on low speed constantly.

With clean beaters, beat the egg whites in a small mixer bowl until foamy. Gradually beat in the remaining 2 tablespoons sugar; continue beating on high speed until the mixture forms soft peaks. Stir about ¼ of the egg white mixture into the cake batter. Fold the rest in gently with a rubber spatula. Pour batter evenly into the prepared springform pan, smoothing top. Bake 25 to 30 minutes or until a wooden toothpick inserted in the center comes out clean. Place cake in pan upright on a wire rack to cool for 10 minutes; then remove cake from pan and continue cooling on rack. Top with Chocolate Frosting (page 128) or Fluffy Divinity Frosting (page 127), if desired. Makes 12 servings.

NUTRITION (PER SERVING): 216 CALORIES

TOTAL FAT	5 g	(22% OF CALORIES)
PROTEIN	3 g	(6% OF CALORIES)
CARBOHYDRATES	39 g	(71% OF CALORIES)
CHOLESTEROL	15 mg	
SODIUM	172 mg	

Pumpkin and Spice Tunnel Cake

¼ cup firmly packed brown sugar
1 cup canned pumpkin or mashed cooked pumpkin
1½ teaspoons pumpkin pie spice
½ teaspoon maple flavoring
1 egg, lightly beaten
1 cup firmly packed brown sugar
¼ cup plus 1 tablespoon vegetable oil
2 egg whites
2¾ cups flour
½ cup oat bran
1¼ teaspoons baking soda
¼ teaspoon salt
1⅓ cups nonfat buttermilk
2 teaspoons vanilla
½ cup confectioner's sugar
2 teaspoons skim milk
½ teaspoon pumpkin pie spice

Preheat oven to 350 degrees F. Spray a 12-cup Bundt pan with nonstick cooking spray; set aside. In a small bowl, combine ¼ cup brown sugar, pumpkin, 1½ teaspoons pumpkin pie spice, maple flavoring, and egg. Stir well and set aside.

In a large mixer bowl, beat together 1 cup brown sugar and oil. Add egg whites and beat well.

Sift together the flour, oat bran, baking soda, and salt. Add to brown sugar mixture alternately with buttermilk. Stir in vanilla. Set aside 2 cups of the batter and pour the rest into the prepared pan. Spoon the pumpkin mixture in a ring over the center of the batter in the pan. Pour reserved batter over pumpkin mixture. Bake for 50 minutes or until a wooden toothpick inserted in center comes out clean. Let stand in pan 10 minutes, then remove from pan and place on a wire rack to cool completely. Combine confectioner's sugar, milk, and ½ teaspoon pumpkin pie spice; mix until smooth. Drizzle over cake. Makes 16 servings.

NUTRITION (PER SERVING): 216 CALORIES

TOTAL FAT	4 g	(18% OF CALORIES)
PROTEIN	4 g	(8% OF CALORIES)
CARBOHYDRATES	40 g	(74% OF CALORIES)
CHOLESTEROL	14 mg	
SODIUM	139 mg	

Gingerbread

1½ cups all-purpose flour
½ cup sugar
2 teaspoons baking powder
1 teaspoon ginger
½ teaspoon cinnamon
¼ teaspoon salt
¼ teaspoon cloves
½ cup boiling water
⅓ cup molasses
¼ cup vegetable oil

Preheat oven to 325 degrees F. Spray an 8-inch square baking pan with nonstick cooking spray; set aside.

Sift together flour, sugar, baking powder, ginger, cinnamon, salt, and cloves into a large mixing bowl. Combine water, molasses, and oil. Pour into flour mixture and beat at medium speed until smooth. Pour batter into prepared pan and bake for 25 to 30 minutes or until a wooden toothpick inserted in center comes out clean. Serve topped with unsweetened applesauce, sliced bananas, or low-fat whipped topping. Makes 16 servings.

NUTRITION (PER SERVING): 121 CALORIES

TOTAL FAT	4 g	(27% OF CALORIES)
PROTEIN	1 g	(4% OF CALORIES)
CARBOHYDRATES	21 g	(69% OF CALORIES)
CHOLESTEROL	0 mg	
SODIUM	88 mg	

Apple Walnut Cake

2 cups flour
1 ¼ cups sugar
1 teaspoon baking soda
1 teaspoon salt
1 teaspoon cinnamon
½ teaspoon baking powder
½ cup vegetable oil
¼ cup apple juice
2 whole eggs
1 egg white
2 cups cubed peeled apples
½ cup chopped walnuts

Preheat oven to 350 degrees F. Spray a 13 x 9-inch baking pan with nonstick cooking spray; set aside.

Sift together the flour, sugar, baking soda, salt, cinnamon, and baking powder into a medium bowl. Make a well in the center of the mixture. Combine oil, apple juice, eggs, and egg white. Pour into well in dry ingredients and stir until moistened. Fold in apple cubes and walnuts. Pour batter into the prepared pan, and bake for 40 minutes or until a wooden toothpick inserted in the center comes out clean. Cool completely in pan. Makes 18 servings.

NUTRITION (PER SERVING): 201 CALORIES

TOTAL FAT	9 g	(40% OF CALORIES)
PROTEIN	3 g	(6% OF CALORIES)
CARBOHYDRATES	28 g	(55% OF CALORIES)
CHOLESTEROL	24 mg	
SODIUM	197 mg	

Carrot Spice Ring

1 cup firmly packed brown sugar
¼ cup vegetable oil
2 eggs
3 cups flour
2 teaspoons baking powder
1 teaspoon baking soda
1 ½ teaspoons cinnamon
½ teaspoon ginger
½ teaspoon allspice
1 cup unsweetened orange juice
½ cup nonfat buttermilk
2 teaspoons vanilla
1 ½ cups finely shredded carrots
⅓ cup confectioner's sugar
¼ cup light cream cheese, softened
¼ teaspoon cinnamon
1 tablespoon skim milk

Preheat oven to 350 degrees F. Spray a 12-cup Bundt pan with nonstick cooking spray; set aside.

In a large mixer bowl, cream together brown sugar and oil. Add eggs, one at a time, beating well after each addition.

Sift together the flour, baking powder, baking soda, cinnamon, ginger, and allspice. Mix orange juice with buttermilk. Add flour to creamed mixture alternately with orange juice mixture, beating constantly to mix well. Add vanilla. Stir in carrots.

Pour batter into prepared pan and bake for 45 minutes or until a wooden toothpick inserted in center comes out clean. Let stand in pan for 10 minutes; then remove to a wire rack to complete cooling.

Mix together confectioner's sugar, cream cheese, and cinnamon; gradually add skim milk until icing reaches desired consistency. Drizzle over cooled cake. Makes 16 servings.

NUTRITION (PER SERVING): 208 CALORIES

TOTAL FAT	5 g	(23% OF CALORIES)
PROTEIN	4 g	(8% OF CALORIES)
CARBOHYDRATES	36 g	(70% OF CALORIES)
CHOLESTEROL	30 mg	
SODIUM	134 mg	

Golden Pecan Cake

⅓ cup butter or margarine
½ cup chopped pecans
1 tablespoon flour
1 cup light corn syrup
½ cup firmly packed brown sugar
1 whole egg
2 egg whites
3 cups flour
¾ teaspoon baking soda
¼ teaspoon salt
1 cup nonfat buttermilk
1 teaspoon vanilla
¼ cup confectioner's sugar
1 tablespoon brown sugar
2 teaspoons skim milk

Preheat oven to 350 degrees F. Spray a 12-cup Bundt pan with nonstick cooking spray; set aside.

In a saucepan over medium heat, melt butter or margarine. Stir in pecans and sauté until browned, about 4 minutes. Pour off butter or margarine into a large mixer bowl. Coat drained pecans with 1 tablespoon flour and set aside. Add corn syrup and ½ cup brown sugar to the butter or margarine. Beat until creamy. Beat in whole egg, then egg whites, beating well after each addition.

Sift together 3 cups flour, baking soda, and salt. Add to creamed mixture alternately with buttermilk. Stir in pecans and vanilla. Pour batter into the prepared pan. Bake for 45 minutes or until a wooden pick inserted in center comes out clean. Let stand in pan for 10 minutes; then remove to a wire rack to complete cooling.

Combine confectioner's sugar and 1 tablespoon brown sugar; gradually add skim milk, beating until mixture reaches desired consistency. Drizzle over cooled cake. Makes 16 servings.

NUTRITION (PER SERVING): 253 CALORIES

TOTAL FAT	7 g	(25% OF CALORIES)
PROTEIN	4 g	(6% OF CALORIES)
CARBOHYDRATES	43 g	(69% OF CALORIES)
CHOLESTEROL	24 mg	
SODIUM	158 mg	

Angel Food Cake

12 egg whites (at room temperature)
¼ teaspoon salt
1½ teaspoons cream of tartar
1½ teaspoons vanilla extract
¼ teaspoon almond extract
1½ cups sugar, divided
1 cup sifted cake flour

Preheat oven to 375 degrees F. Beat egg whites and salt in a large bowl at high speed until foamy. Add cream of tartar, vanilla, and almond extract. Beat until soft peaks form. Gradually add ¾ cup sugar, 1 tablespoon at a time, beating until stiff peaks form.

Sift flour and remaining ¾ cup sugar together 3 times. Sift flour mixture over egg-white mixture, one-fourth at a time. Fold well after each addition.

Spoon batter into an ungreased 10-inch tube pan. Bake for 30 to 35 minutes or until cake springs back when lightly touched. Invert pan and let cake cool completely in pan. Run knife around edge to loosen cake before removing from pan. Garnish with fresh fruit, if desired. Makes 16 servings.

NUTRITION (PER SERVING): 111 CALORIES

TOTAL FAT	0 g	(0% OF CALORIES)
PROTEIN	3 g	(12% OF CALORIES)
CARBOHYDRATES	24 g	(88% OF CALORIES)
CHOLESTEROL	0 mg	
SODIUM	100 mg	

Banana Nut Fudge Cake

1½ cups sugar

½ cup shortening

3 eggs

1 teaspoon almond extract

1 teaspoon vanilla

1½ cups flour

½ cup cocoa

1 teaspoon baking soda

½ teaspoon salt

½ cup toasted chopped almonds or pistachios

1½ cups pureed ripe bananas (about 3 medium)

Preheat oven to 350 degrees F. Spray a 12-cup Bundt pan with nonstick cooking spray; set aside.

In a large mixer bowl, cream together sugar and shortening. Add eggs, almond extract, and vanilla; beat until fluffy.

Sift together flour, cocoa, baking soda, and salt. Stir in nuts. Add flour mixture to creamed mixture alternately with pureed bananas, mixing well. Pour batter into prepared pan and bake for 50 minutes or until toothpick inserted in center comes out clean and cake pulls away from sides of pan. Let stand in pan 10 minutes, then remove from pan and place on a wire rack to cool completely. Drizzle with Chocolate Glaze (page 127), if desired. Makes 16 servings.

NUTRITION (PER SERVING): 224 CALORIES

TOTAL FAT	8 g	(32% OF CALORIES)
PROTEIN	3 g	(5% OF CALORIES)
CARBOHYDRATES	35 g	(63% OF CALORIES)
CHOLESTEROL	35 mg	
SODIUM	142 mg	

Black Forest Cherry Cake

4 ounces semisweet or German's sweet chocolate

1⅓ cups sugar

¼ cup vegetable oil

4 egg whites

3¼ cups flour

1¼ teaspoons baking soda

¼ teaspoon salt

⅓ cup cocoa

1⅔ cups nonfat buttermilk

2 teaspoons vanilla

1 can (21 ounces) light cherry pie filling

¼ teaspoon almond extract

Preheat oven to 350 degrees F. Spray a 12-cup Bundt pan with nonstick cooking spray; set aside.

Melt chocolate in the top of a double boiler or in microwave. In a large mixer bowl, cream together sugar and oil; add melted chocolate and beat well. Beat in egg whites.

Sift together flour, baking soda, salt, and cocoa. Add to creamed mixture alternately with buttermilk, beating well. Add vanilla. Set aside 2 cups of the batter and pour the remainder into the prepared pan.

Mix cherry pie filling with almond extract and spoon in a ring over the center of the batter in the pan. Pour reserved batter over pie filling. Bake for 55 minutes or until a wooden toothpick inserted in center comes out clean. Let stand in pan 10 minutes, then remove from pan and place on a wire rack to cool completely. Drizzle with Chocolate Glaze (page 127), if desired. Makes 16 servings.

NUTRITION (PER SERVING): 293 CALORIES

TOTAL FAT	6 g	(19% OF CALORIES)
PROTEIN	5 g	(7% OF CALORIES)
CARBOHYDRATES	54 g	(73% OF CALORIES)
CHOLESTEROL	1 mg	
SODIUM	159 mg	

Fresh Strawberry Pie (page 137), Lime Chiffon Pie (page 139), Swiss Apple-Cherry Pie (page 138)

Lemon Glaze

1½ cups confectioner's sugar
2 tablespoons skim milk
1 teaspoon finely shredded lemon peel
2 teaspoons lemon juice

In a small bowl stir together confectioner's sugar, milk, lemon peel, and lemon juice until smooth and of drizzling consistency. Makes 16 servings.

NUTRITION (PER SERVING): 48 CALORIES

TOTAL FAT	0 g	(0% OF CALORIES)
PROTEIN	0 g	(1% OF CALORIES)
CARBOHYDRATES	12 g	(99% OF CALORIES)
CHOLESTEROL	0 mg	
SODIUM	0 mg	

Chocolate Glaze

1 cup sifted confectioner's sugar
2 tablespoons cocoa
2 tablespoons skim milk
½ teaspoon vanilla

In a small bowl stir together sifted confectioner's sugar, cocoa, milk, and vanilla until smooth. Add a few drops of milk, if needed, to achieve desired consistency. Makes 16 servings.

NUTRITION (PER SERVING): 33 CALORIES

TOTAL FAT	0 g	(0% OF CALORIES)
PROTEIN	0 g	(1% OF CALORIES)
CARBOHYDRATES	8 g	(99% OF CALORIES)
CHOLESTEROL	0 mg	
SODIUM	12 mg	

Fluffy Divinity Frosting

Pictured on cover.

½ cup water
1½ cup sugar
2 egg whites
½ teaspoon cream of tartar
2 teaspoons vanilla

Combine water and sugar in a medium-sized heavy saucepan. Stir over low heat until sugar is dissolved. Turn heat to high and bring mixture to a boil. Continue boiling over medium heat, without stirring, until syrup reaches hard-ball stage (265 degrees F. on candy thermometer).

Meanwhile, beat egg whites in the large bowl of an electric mixer until soft peaks form. Remove syrup from stove and pour about ⅓ of it into the egg whites in a thin stream, beating constantly on high speed. Return remaining syrup mixture to stove and cook an additional 2 to 3 minutes, or until it reaches soft-crack stage (275 degrees F. on candy thermometer). Pour remaining syrup into egg-white mixture in a thin stream, beating constantly. Beat until stiff peaks form. Makes 12 servings.

NUTRITION (PER SERVING): 104 CALORIES

TOTAL FAT	0 g	(0% OF CALORIES)
PROTEIN	1 g	(4% OF CALORIES)
CARBOHYDRATES	25 g	(96% OF CALORIES)
CHOLESTEROL	0 mg	
SODIUM	10 mg	

Chocolate Frosting

⅓ cup cocoa
3 cups confectioner's sugar
¼ cup light butter or margarine, softened
2 tablespoons skim milk
1 teaspoon vanilla

Combine cocoa and confectioner's sugar in a small mixing bowl. Add butter or margarine, milk, and vanilla. Beat until smooth, adding additional milk a few drops at a time, if needed. Makes 12 servings.

NUTRITION (PER SERVING):   139 CALORIES

TOTAL FAT	2 g	(13% OF CALORIES)
PROTEIN	0 g	(0% OF CALORIES)
CARBOHYDRATES	30 g	(87% OF CALORIES)
CHOLESTEROL	5 mg	
SODIUM	25 mg	

Ginger Chews

Pictured on page 107.

⅓ cup light butter, softened
⅔ cup firmly packed brown sugar
1 teaspoon baking soda
1 teaspoon ginger
½ teaspoon cinnamon
1 egg
¼ cup dark molasses
1½ cups white flour
½ cup whole wheat flour
¼ cup granulated sugar
1 teaspoon cinnamon

Spray cookie sheet with nonstick cooking spray; set aside. In a large mixing bowl, beat the butter with an electric mixer on medium to high speed for 30 seconds. Add the brown sugar, baking soda, ginger, and ½ teaspoon cinnamon; beat until combined. Beat in egg and molasses. Beat in as much of the white and whole wheat flours as you can with the mixer. Stir in any remaining flour with a wooden spoon. Cover and chill in the refrigerator for 1 hour.

Shape dough into 1-inch balls. Combine the granulated sugar and 1 teaspoon cinnamon. Roll balls in sugar-cinnamon mixture. Place 2 inches apart on prepared cookie sheet. Bake at 350 degrees F. for 10 to 11 minutes or until tops of cookies are cracked. (Cookies are best if slightly underbaked.) Remove from cookie sheet and cool on wire racks. Makes about 4 dozen cookies.

NUTRITION (PER COOKIE):   41 CALORIES

TOTAL FAT	1 g	(19% OF CALORIES)
PROTEIN	1 g	(7% OF CALORIES)
CARBOHYDRATES	8 g	(74% OF CALORIES)
CHOLESTEROL	6 mg	
SODIUM	28 mg	

Chocolate Sprinkle Cookies

¼ cup butter or margarine
¼ cup granulated sugar
¼ cup firmly packed brown sugar
1 egg white
1 whole egg
1 tablespoon vanilla
1¼ cups white flour
¼ cup whole wheat flour
½ teaspoon baking soda
1 ounce (1 square) semisweet baking
    chocolate, grated

In a large mixing bowl, cream together the butter or margarine, granulated sugar, and brown sugar. Add egg white, whole egg, and vanilla; beat until fluffy. Stir together the flours and baking soda; add to creamed mixture, stirring with a wooden spoon to blend thoroughly. Add grated chocolate and mix well.

Drop dough by rounded teaspoonfuls about 2 inches apart onto ungreased cookie sheets. Bake at 375 degrees F. for 6 to 8 minutes or until lightly browned around the edges. Remove immediately from cookie sheets and cool on wire racks. Makes about 3 dozen cookies.

NUTRITION (PER COOKIE):   48 CALORIES

TOTAL FAT	2 g	(33% OF CALORIES)
PROTEIN	1 g	(7% OF CALORIES)
CARBOHYDRATES	7 g	(60% OF CALORIES)
CHOLESTEROL	9 mg	
SODIUM	28 mg	

Chocolate Meringue Cookies

2 egg whites, at room temperature
⅛ teaspoon salt
¼ teaspoon cream of tartar
½ cup sugar
½ teaspoon vinegar
½ teaspoon vanilla
¼ cup cocoa
1 tablespoon cornstarch

Preheat oven to 250 degrees F. Using an electric mixer on high speed, beat egg whites and salt until foamy. Sprinkle in cream of tartar and continue beating until soft peaks form. Without stopping mixer, add sugar very gradually. Beat about 10 minutes more or until mixture is glossy and stands in stiff peaks. Beat in vinegar and vanilla just until blended. Stir together the cocoa and cornstarch and fold the mixture gently into the egg white mixture with a spoon.

Line a cookie sheet with unglazed brown paper. Drop mixture by tablespoons onto the paper. Place in oven; immediately reduce oven temperature to 225 degrees F., and bake for 1½ hours or until meringue is dry. Turn oven off, but leave door closed. Let cookies stand undisturbed in oven for 1 hour. Remove cookies carefully from brown paper and store in an airtight container. Makes about 2 dozen cookies.

NUTRITION (PER COOKIE):   23 CALORIES

TOTAL FAT	LESS THAN 1 g	(5% OF CALORIES)
PROTEIN	LESS THAN 1 g	(8% OF CALORIES)
CARBOHYDRATES	5 g	(87% OF CALORIES)
CHOLESTEROL	0 mg	
SODIUM	51 mg	

Applesauce Oatmeal Cookies

1 cup firmly packed brown sugar
¾ cup plus 2 tablespoons applesauce
1 egg white
1 tablespoon vanilla
1 cup rolled oats
2½ cups flour
1 teaspoon baking soda
1 teaspoon cinnamon
¼ teaspoon salt
1 cup raisins

Spray cookie sheets with nonstick cooking spray; set aside.

Mix brown sugar, applesauce, egg white, and vanilla until well blended. Stir together oats, flour, baking soda, cinnamon, and salt; add to applesauce mixture. Fold in raisins. Drop by spoonfuls 2 inches apart onto prepared cookie sheets. Bake at 350 degrees F. for 15 minutes. Remove from cookie sheet and cool on wire rack. Makes about 4 dozen cookies.

NUTRITION (PER COOKIE): 70 CALORIES

TOTAL FAT	LESS THAN 1 g	(3% OF CALORIES)
PROTEIN	1 g	(6% OF CALORIES)
CARBOHYDRATES	16 g	(91% OF CALORIES)
CHOLESTEROL	9 mg	
SODIUM	122 mg	

Gingerbread Cut-Out Cookies

⅔ cup firmly packed brown sugar
⅓ cup butter or margarine
1 egg white
⅓ cup light molasses
3 tablespoons light corn syrup
1 teaspoon vanilla
3 cups flour
1½ teaspoons ginger
1¼ teaspoons cinnamon
1¼ teaspoons baking powder
¾ teaspoon baking soda
⅛ teaspoon cloves
⅛ teaspoon salt

Cream together brown sugar and butter or margarine. Add egg white, molasses, corn syrup, and vanilla; continue beating until thoroughly blended. Sift together flour, ginger, cinnamon, baking powder, baking soda, cloves, and salt. Gradually beat about half this mixture into creamed mixture. Stir in the rest of the dry ingredients with a wooden spoon until well mixed. Divide dough in half and wrap each half in plastic wrap. Chill in refrigerator until firm, at least 1 hour.

When ready to bake, preheat oven to 375 degrees F. Lightly spray cookie sheets with nonstick cooking spray; set aside. Work with one portion of the dough, leaving remaining half in refrigerator. On a lightly floured work surface, roll out the dough about ¼-inch thick, using flour as needed to keep rolling pin from sticking. Cut cookies into desired shapes and transfer to prepared cookie sheets with a large spatula. Repeat with second half of dough. Combine scraps and chill again if necessary until firm. Repeat rolling and cutting until all the dough is used. Bake for 7 to 9 minutes or until edges are lightly browned. (Do not overbake.) Makes about 3 dozen cookies.

NUTRITION (PER COOKIE): 88 CALORIES

TOTAL FAT	2 g	(19% OF CALORIES)
PROTEIN	1 g	(6% OF CALORIES)
CARBOHYDRATES	17 g	(76% OF CALORIES)
CHOLESTEROL	5 mg	
SODIUM	61 mg	

Oatmeal Crisps

½ cup butter or margarine, softened
1 cup granulated sugar
1 cup firmly packed brown sugar
1 teaspoon vanilla
1 whole egg
1 egg white
2¼ cups flour
1¼ teaspoons baking powder
1¼ teaspoons baking soda
¼ cup 1% low-fat milk
2 cups rolled oats
2 cups crisp rice cereal
½ cup raisins

Preheat oven to 325 degrees F. Spray cookie sheets with nonstick cooking spray; set aside.

In a large bowl, cream together until fluffy the butter or margarine, sugars, and vanilla. Add egg and egg white. Beat well.

Sift together flour, baking powder, and baking soda. Add to creamed mixture alternately with milk, mixing well. Stir in oats, rice cereal, and raisins. Drop by heaping teaspoonfuls about 2 inches apart onto prepared cookie sheets. Bake for 15 to 18 minutes or until lightly browned. Remove from pans and cool on wire racks. Makes about 6 dozen cookies.

NUTRITION (PER COOKIE):   60 CALORIES

TOTAL FAT	1 g	(22% OF CALORIES)
PROTEIN	1 g	(7% OF CALORIES)
CARBOHYDRATES	11 g	(71% OF CALORIES)
CHOLESTEROL	9 mg	
SODIUM	93 mg	

Coconut Kisses

3 egg whites, at room temperature
1 teaspoon vanilla
1 cup sugar
2 cups sweetened flaked coconut

Preheat oven to 325 degrees F. Spray cookie sheets with nonstick cooking spray; set aside.

In a large mixer bowl, beat egg whites and vanilla on high speed of electric mixer until soft peaks form. Gradually add sugar, and beat until stiff peaks form. Fold in coconut gently. Drop by spoonfuls 2 inches apart onto prepared cookie sheets. Bake 20 minutes or until very lightly browned. Remove from pans to wire racks to cool. Makes about 30 cookies.

NUTRITION (PER COOKIE):   62 CALORIES

TOTAL FAT	2 g	(29% OF CALORIES)
PROTEIN	1 g	(6% OF CALORIES)
CARBOHYDRATES	10 g	(65% OF CALORIES)
CHOLESTEROL	0 mg	
SODIUM	3 mg	

Brownies

Pictured on page 107.

½ cup nonfat plain yogurt
⅔ cup sugar
1 teaspoon vanilla
1 cup flour
¼ cup cocoa
2 teaspoons baking powder
½ teaspoon baking soda
½ cup cold water
2 egg whites

Preheat oven to 350 degrees F. Spray a 9-inch square cake pan with nonstick cooking spray; set aside.

In a large mixing bowl, combine yogurt, sugar, and vanilla, and beat on high speed for two minutes. Stir or sift together flour, cocoa, baking powder, and baking soda. Add to yogurt mixture alternately with cold water, beating until well combined.

Using clean beaters, beat the egg whites in a small mixing bowl until stiff peaks form. Gently fold the beaten egg whites into the cake batter and pour into prepared pan. Bake for 30 minutes or until set. Cool in pan for 10 minutes, then remove to wire rack to complete cooling. Dust with confectioner's sugar, if desired. Makes 12 servings.

NUTRITION (PER SERVING): 97 CALORIES

TOTAL FAT	0 g	(3% OF CALORIES)
PROTEIN	3 g	(10% OF CALORIES)
CARBOHYDRATES	21 g	(86% OF CALORIES)
CHOLESTEROL	0 mg	
SODIUM	122 mg	

Strawberry Shortbread Bars

1¼ cups flour
3 tablespoons sugar
¼ cup light butter
1 egg white
½ teaspoon finely shredded fresh lemon peel
1 tablespoon water
¼ cup low-calorie strawberry preserves
½ cup sifted confectioner's sugar
2 teaspoons lemon juice

In a medium mixing bowl, stir together the flour and sugar. Cut in light butter with a fork or pastry blender until mixture resembles fine crumbs. Stir in egg white, lemon peel, and water. If dough is too crumbly, add an additional 1 tablespoon water. Form into a ball and knead until smooth. Divide dough in half. Shape each portion into an 8-inch log. Place the logs 4 to 5 inches apart on an ungreased cookie sheet. Pat each log into a 2-inch-wide strip. Using the back of a spoon, slightly press a 1-inch-wide indentation lengthwise down the center of each strip.

Bake at 325 degrees F. for 20 to 25 minutes or until edges are light brown. Place cookie sheet on a wire rack. If necessary, reshape the indentations in the shortbread by pressing with a spoon. Immediately spoon strawberry spread into the indentations. While shortbread is still warm, cut the strips crosswise on the diagonal into 1-inch-wide pieces. Remove from pan and cool on wire rack.

While cookies are cooling, stir together confectioner's sugar and enough lemon juice to make an icing of drizzling consistency. Drizzle over cooled bars. Makes 14 bars.

NUTRITION (PER SERVING): 99 CALORIES

TOTAL FAT	2 g	(17% OF CALORIES)
PROTEIN	1 g	(6% OF CALORIES)
CARBOHYDRATES	19 g	(78% OF CALORIES)
CHOLESTEROL	4 mg	
SODIUM	25 mg	

Lemon Bars

¾ cup flour
3 tablespoons sugar
¼ cup light butter
1 whole egg
1 egg white
⅔ cup sugar
2 tablespoons flour
¼ teaspoon finely shredded lemon peel
2 tablespoons lemon juice
1 tablespoon water
¼ teaspoon baking powder
1 tablespoon confectioner's sugar

Preheat oven to 350 degrees F. Spray an 8-inch square baking pan with nonstick cooking spray; set aside.

In a small mixing bowl, combine ¾ cup flour and 3 tablespoons sugar. Cut in light butter with a fork or pastry blender until crumbly. Pat mixture onto the bottom of the prepared pan. Bake for 15 minutes.

Meanwhile, in the same bowl combine egg and egg white. Beat with an electric mixer on medium speed until frothy. Add ⅔ cup sugar, 2 tablespoons flour, lemon peel, lemon juice, water, and baking powder. Beat on medium speed for 3 minutes or until slightly thickened. Pour mixture over baked layer in pan. Bake for 20 to 25 minutes more or until edges are light brown and center is set. Cool in pan on a wire rack. Sift confectioner's sugar over top. Cut into bars. Store in refrigerator. Makes 16 bars.

NUTRITION (PER SERVING): 88 CALORIES

TOTAL FAT	2 g	(19% OF CALORIES)
PROTEIN	1 g	(6% OF CALORIES)
CARBOHYDRATES	17 g	(75% OF CALORIES)
CHOLESTEROL	17 mg	
SODIUM	30 mg	

Blondie Bars

½ cup light butter, softened
½ cup granulated sugar
½ cup firmly packed brown sugar
1 teaspoon baking soda
¼ teaspoon salt
½ cup unsweetened applesauce
1 egg
1 teaspoon vanilla
2¼ cups flour
½ cup miniature semisweet chocolate chips

Preheat oven to 350 degrees F. Spray a 13 x 9-inch baking pan with nonstick cooking spray; set aside.

In a large mixing bowl, cream together the butter, sugars, baking soda, and salt. Beat until light and fluffy. Beat in the applesauce, egg, and vanilla. Beat in as much of the flour as you can with the mixer. Stir in any remaining flour with a wooden spoon. Stir in the chocolate chips. Spread dough into the prepared baking pan. Bake for 20 to 25 minutes or until light brown and a wooden toothpick inserted in center comes out clean. Cool thoroughly in pan on wire rack. Cut into bars. Makes 36.

NUTRITION (PER SERVING): 74 CALORIES

TOTAL FAT	2 g	(29% OF CALORIES)
PROTEIN	1 g	(6% OF CALORIES)
CARBOHYDRATES	12 g	(65% OF CALORIES)
CHOLESTEROL	9 mg	
SODIUM	57 mg	

Raisin Squares

1 cup raisins (seeded raisins are best)
1½ cups water
2 tablespoons margarine
2 cups flour
1 cup sugar
1 teaspoon baking powder
1 teaspoon baking soda
1 teaspoon salt
1 teaspoon cinnamon
½ teaspoon nutmeg
1 cup chopped nuts (optional)

Preheat oven to 350 degrees F. Spray a 13 x 9-inch baking pan with nonstick cooking spray; set aside.

Combine raisins and water in a medium saucepan. Boil uncovered until 1 cup of liquid remains. Add margarine to raisin mixture; stir to melt. In a large bowl, combine flour, sugar, baking powder, baking soda, salt, cinnamon, nutmeg, and nuts. Add raisin mixture and mix until well combined. Spread in the prepared pan and bake for 18 to 20 minutes or until golden brown. Spread with Lemon Glaze (page 127), if desired. Cut into bars. Makes 30.

NUTRITION (PER SERVING): 81 CALORIES

TOTAL FAT	1 g	(10% OF CALORIES)
PROTEIN	1 g	(5% OF CALORIES)
CARBOHYDRATES	17 g	(85% OF CALORIES)
CHOLESTEROL	0 mg	
SODIUM	128 mg	

Sugar-Free Raisin Bars

1 cup raisins
½ cup water
¼ cup butter or margarine
1 teaspoon cinnamon
¼ teaspoon nutmeg
1 cup flour
1 egg
¾ cup unsweetened applesauce
1 tablespoon sugar substitute
1 teaspoon baking soda
¼ teaspoon vanilla

Preheat oven to 350 degrees F. Spray an 8-inch square pan with nonstick cooking spray; set aside.

Combine raisins, water, butter or margarine, cinnamon, and nutmeg in a medium saucepan. Cook over medium heat, stirring frequently, until butter or margarine is melted; continue cooking for 3 minutes. Stir in flour, egg, applesauce, sugar substitute, baking soda, and vanilla. Spread mixture in prepared pan. Bake for 25 to 30 minutes or until lightly browned. Cool and cut into bars. Makes 16.

NUTRITION (PER SERVING): 102 CALORIES

TOTAL FAT	3 g	(30% OF CALORIES)
PROTEIN	2 g	(6% OF CALORIES)
CARBOHYDRATES	16 g	(64% OF CALORIES)
CHOLESTEROL	21 mg	
SODIUM	86 mg	

Date Bars with Orange Icing

Pictured on page 107.

1 cup flour
1 teaspoon baking powder
½ teaspoon cinnamon
¼ teaspoon baking soda
½ cup snipped dates
1 cup boiling water
2 eggs
1 cup firmly packed brown sugar
¾ cup evaporated skim milk
¼ cup finely chopped toasted walnuts
2 cups confectioner's sugar
2 tablespoons light butter, softened
2 tablespoons orange juice
½ teaspoon finely shredded orange peel

Preheat oven to 350 degrees F. Spray a 13 x 9-inch baking pan with nonstick cooking spray; set aside.

Stir or sift together flour, baking powder, cinnamon, and baking soda. Set aside.

Place dates in a small bowl and pour boiling water over them. Let stand for 10 minutes. Drain well. In a large mixing bowl, beat eggs with an electric mixer on high speed until frothy. Add brown sugar and dates, beating until mixture is well combined. Stir in evaporated skim milk.

Add flour mixture to egg mixture, stirring with a wooden spoon to mix well. Stir in nuts. Pour batter into the prepared pan. Bake for about 20 minutes or until top springs back when touched lightly with finger. Cool in pan on a wire rack.

While bars are cooling, combine confectioner's sugar, butter, orange juice, and orange peel, stirring until smooth. Spread over cooled date bars in pan; cut into bars. Makes 24.

NUTRITION (PER SERVING):   114 CALORIES

TOTAL FAT	2 g	(16% OF CALORIES)
PROTEIN	2 g	(7% OF CALORIES)
CARBOHYDRATES	22 g	(77% OF CALORIES)
CHOLESTEROL	18 mg	
SODIUM	40 mg	

Chocolate Cookie Cups

¼ cup firmly packed brown sugar
2 tablespoons light corn syrup
2 tablespoons light butter
¼ cup all-purpose flour
1 tablespoon finely chopped toasted walnuts

Preheat oven to 350 degrees F. Spray cookie sheets with nonstick cooking spray; set aside.

In a small saucepan, combine brown sugar, corn syrup, and light butter. Cook and stir over medium heat until mixture boils. Remove from heat. Stir in flour and walnuts; beat until smooth.

Spoon 1 level tablespoon batter for each cookie, about 6 inches apart, onto prepared cookie sheet. Place only 2 cookies on each sheet. Bake for 6 to 8 minutes or until cookies are just set. Remove from oven and let cool on cookie sheet 1 to 2 minutes, until set but still flexible. (If cookies become too firm, return to oven for 15 to 20 seconds.)

Remove cookies from sheet and drape over inverted 6-ounce custard cups to finish cooling. Let cookie sheet cool, and spray again with nonstick cooking spray before making 2 more cookies. To serve, place scoops of nonfat frozen yogurt in cups. Makes 8 cookie cups.

NUTRITION (PER COOKIE):   66 CALORIES

TOTAL FAT	2 g	(27% OF CALORIES)
PROTEIN	1 g	(6% OF CALORIES)
CARBOHYDRATES	11 g	(67% OF CALORIES)
CHOLESTEROL	0 mg	
SODIUM	43 mg	

PIES AND DESSERTS

Lite Pie Crust

⅓ cup margarine, cut in small pieces
1 cup flour
⅓ cup ice water
1 egg white
1½ teaspoons white vinegar
¼ teaspoon salt

In a small bowl, cut margarine into flour with a fork until mixture resembles coarse meal. Combine water, egg white, vinegar, and salt in a small bowl; mix well. Add liquid mixture to flour mixture. Mix lightly with a fork until mixture forms a ball. Refrigerate for at least ½ hour before rolling out dough. Makes one 9-inch pie shell, or pastry for a 1-crust pie.

For baked pie shell: Roll pastry in a circle; fit into pie tin. Flute edges. Prick in several places with fork. Bake at 425 degrees F. for 12 to 15 minutes or until light golden brown. Makes 8 servings.

NUTRITION (PER SERVING): 112 CALORIES

TOTAL FAT	7 g	(55% OF CALORIES)
PROTEIN	2 g	(7% OF CALORIES)
CARBOHYDRATES	12 g	(38% OF CALORIES)
CHOLESTEROL	0 mg	
SODIUM	170 mg	

Fresh Strawberry Pie

Pictured on page 125.

1 Lite Pie Crust baked pie shell (see opposite column)
3 cups water
1 cup sugar
1 package (3 ounces) strawberry-flavored gelatin
3 tablespoons cornstarch
3 cups fresh strawberries, washed and hulled

Prepare 1 Lite Pie Crust baked pie shell according to directions (opposite column). In a medium saucepan, bring water and sugar to boil. Mix gelatin with cornstarch; gradually add to boiling mixture. Cook over medium-high heat, stirring constantly, for 5 minutes or until mixture is clear and thickened slightly. Let stand at room temperature until just warm, about 15 minutes. Pour over fresh strawberries and fold together gently. Mound in baked pie shell. Chill for at least 1 hour before serving. Top with low-fat whipped topping, if desired. Makes 8 servings.

NUTRITION (PER SERVING): 300 CALORIES

TOTAL FAT	8 g	(24% OF CALORIES)
PROTEIN	3 g	(4% OF CALORIES)
CARBOHYDRATES	54 g	(72% OF CALORIES)
CHOLESTEROL	0 mg	
SODIUM	193 mg	

Swiss Apple-Cherry Pie

Pictured on page 125.

2 batches Lite Pie Crust pie dough (see page 137)
3 medium Granny Smith apples
2 tablespoons light butter
1 cup sugar
2 tablespoons flour
2 teaspoons cinnamon
½ teaspoon nutmeg
1½ cups pitted tart cherries, drained
Evaporated skim milk
½ teaspoon sugar
¼ teaspoon cinnamon

Prepare a double batch of Lite Pie Crust according to directions (page 137). Roll out ½ of the dough and line a 9-inch pie tin with it.

Pare apples; core and slice. Melt butter and brush on bottom of pastry shell. Mix together 1 cup sugar, flour, 2 teaspoons cinnamon, and nutmeg. Stir half of this mixture into the cherries, and toss the other half with apple slices. Arrange cherries on the bottom of the pastry shell. Place apples in a layer over the cherries. Roll out second half of dough for top crust. Cut two 2-inch slits near center (or make a fancier cut-out design, if desired). Moisten the edge of the bottom crust around the rim. Place top crust carefully over pie; trim, leaving ½ inch to extend over rim. Press top and bottom crusts together and flute around rim. Make sure slits are open to allow steam to escape while cooking. After top crust is placed on pie, brush crust with evaporated milk and sprinkle ½ teaspoon sugar mixed with ¼ teaspoon cinnamon over top. Bake at 425 degrees F. for 30 to 40 minutes. Makes 8 servings.

NUTRITION (PER SERVING): 339 CALORIES

TOTAL FAT	15 g	(40% OF CALORIES)
PROTEIN	2 g	(8% OF CALORIES)
CARBOHYDRATES	49 g	(58% OF CALORIES)
CHOLESTEROL	5 mg	
SODIUM	363 mg	

Sugar-Free Apple Pie

½ cup low-fat ricotta cheese
5 packets artificial sweetener
3 tablespoons skim milk
1 egg white
2 tablespoons vegetable oil
1½ teaspoons vanilla
1 dash salt
2 cups flour
2 teaspoons baking powder
2 tablespoons water
6 medium apples
¼ cup flour
½ teaspoon cinnamon
12 packets artificial sweetener

Preheat oven to 375 degrees F. Mix together the ricotta cheese, 5 packets sweetener, milk, egg white, oil, vanilla, and salt. Add 2 cups flour, baking powder, and water and mix until dough forms. Divide pastry into two equal pieces; wrap and place in refrigerator to chill.

Roll out half of the pie dough and line a 9-inch pie tin. Peel and slice apples. Toss apples with ¼ cup flour, cinnamon, and 12 packets sweetener. Arrange in pie shell. Roll out second half of dough for top crust. Cut two 2-inch slits near center (or make a fancier cut-out design, if desired). Moisten the edge of the bottom crust around the rim. Place top crust carefully over pie; trim, leaving ½ inch to extend over rim. Press top and bottom crusts together and flute around rim. Make sure slits are open to allow steam to escape while cooking.

Bake at 375 degrees F. for 20 minutes, then reduce oven temperature to 325 degrees F. and bake 25 minutes longer. Makes 8 servings.

NUTRITION (PER SERVING): 314 CALORIES

TOTAL FAT	6 g	(16% OF CALORIES)
PROTEIN	6 g	(8% OF CALORIES)
CARBOHYDRATES	59 g	(76% OF CALORIES)
CHOLESTEROL	5 mg	
SODIUM	166 mg	

Lime Chiffon Pie

Pictured on page 125.

1 Lite Pie Crust baked pie shell (see page 137)
1/4 cup sugar
1 envelope unflavored gelatin
1/2 cup water
1/4 cup lime juice
2 egg yolks
1 teaspoon finely shredded lime peel
Green food coloring, if desired
3 egg whites
1/4 cup sugar
1 envelope powdered dessert topping
1/2 cup skim milk

Prepare 1 Lite Pie Crust baked pie shell according to directions (page 137). Cool on a wire rack.

In a medium saucepan, combine 1/4 cup sugar and gelatin. Add water and lime juice. Cook and stir over low heat until gelatin is completely dissolved. Gradually stir the gelatin mixture into the egg yolks. Then return all of the egg yolk mixture to the saucepan. Bring to a gentle boil; cook and stir 2 minutes more. Remove from heat. Cool slightly. Stir in lime peel and food coloring. Cover and chill until mixture is the consistency of syrup, stirring occasionally.

In a medium bowl, beat the egg whites with an electric mixer on medium speed until soft peaks form. Gradually add 1/4 cup sugar, beating on high speed until stiff peaks form. Fold egg whites into slightly thickened gelatin.

Using clean beaters, beat dessert topping with milk according to package directions. Fold the whipped topping into the gelatin mixture. If necessary, chill the filling until it mounds when spooned (about 1 hour). Spoon the filling into the baked pie shell. Cover and chill at least 4 hours (or overnight, if desired), until set. Makes 8 servings.

NUTRITION (PER SERVING): 194 CALORIES

TOTAL FAT	9 g	(41% OF CALORIES)
PROTEIN	5 g	(10% OF CALORIES)
CARBOHYDRATES	24 g	(50% OF CALORIES)
CHOLESTEROL	52 mg	
SODIUM	169 mg	

Lemon Meringue Pie

1 Lite Pie Crust baked pie shell (see page 137)
3/4 cup sugar
1/3 cup cornstarch
1 tablespoon very finely grated lemon peel
1 egg yolk
7 tablespoons lemon juice
1/3 cup orange juice
1 1/3 cups boiling water
4 egg whites, at room temperature
1/2 teaspoon cream of tartar
1 pinch salt
1/3 cup sugar
1/2 teaspoon vanilla

Prepare 1 Lite Pie Crust baked pie shell according to directions (page 137). Cool on a wire rack.

Combine 3/4 cup sugar, cornstarch, and lemon peel in a medium saucepan. Add egg yolk, lemon juice, and orange juice and mix well. Stirring constantly, add boiling water very gradually. Place pan on stove over medium-high heat and cook, stirring constantly, until mixture comes to a boil. Continue cooking, stirring briskly and scraping bottom of pan, for 3 minutes. Remove from heat and pour into prepared pie shell.

In a large mixer bowl, beat egg whites with cream of tartar and salt until very soft peaks begin to form. Add 1/3 cup sugar very gradually, beating constantly until mixture is smooth and stands in soft peaks. Beat in vanilla. Spread meringue over filling in a swirling motion, being sure to seal edges all the way around.

Bake in the lower third of the oven for 15 to 18 minutes or until meringue is nicely browned. Transfer to a wire rack and let stand until cool. Refrigerate until chilled, at least 1 hour. Makes 8 servings.

NUTRITION (PER SERVING): 275 CALORIES

TOTAL FAT	7 g	(22% OF CALORIES)
PROTEIN	4 g	(4% OF CALORIES)
CARBOHYDRATES	49 g	(74% OF CALORIES)
CHOLESTEROL	26 mg	
SODIUM	230 mg	

Blueberry Pie

2 batches Lite Pie Crust pie dough (see page 137)
¼ cup quick-cooking tapioca
¼ cup granulated sugar
2 tablespoons brown sugar
¼ teaspoon salt
⅛ teaspoon cinnamon
3 cups fresh or frozen blueberries, thawed and
    drained (about two 12-ounce packages)*
1 tablespoon lemon juice
1 tablespoon light butter

Prepare a double batch of Lite Pie Crust according to directions (page 137). Roll out half of the dough and line a 9-inch pie tin with it.

Combine tapioca, sugars, salt, cinnamon, blueberries, and lemon juice. Pour into pastry shell. Dot with light butter.

Roll out second half of dough for top crust. Cut two 2-inch slits near center (or make a fancier cut-out design, if desired). Moisten the edge of the bottom crust around the rim. Place top crust carefully over pie; trim, leaving ½ inch to extend over rim. Press top and bottom crusts together and flute around rim. Make sure slits are open to allow steam to escape while cooking. Bake at 425 degrees F. about 45 minutes, or until syrup boils with heavy bubbles and crust is golden brown. Makes 8 servings.

*Note: Canned blueberries may be substituted for fresh or frozen. Use 2 cans (14 ounces each) blueberries, drained. Reduce tapioca to 3 tablespoons.

NUTRITION (PER SERVING): 360 CALORIES

TOTAL FAT	16 g	(40% OF CALORIES)
PROTEIN	5 g	(6% OF CALORIES)
CARBOHYDRATES	49 g	(54% OF CALORIES)
CHOLESTEROL	2 mg	
SODIUM	414 mg	

Peppermint Pie

3 tablespoons light butter, melted
1½ cups crushed chocolate wafer cookies
    (about 16 wafers)
4½ teaspoons sugar
3 cups miniature marshmallows
⅔ cup skim milk
¼ teaspoon peppermint extract
Red food coloring, if desired
2 egg whites
3 tablespoons sugar
1 cup low-fat frozen whipped topping, thawed

Preheat oven to 375 degrees F. Melt butter in a small saucepan. Remove from heat and stir in crushed cookies and 4½ teaspoons sugar. Press mixture into bottom and sides of a 9-inch pie tin. Bake for 5 minutes. Cool.

In a medium saucepan, combine marshmallows and milk. Place over medium heat and cook, stirring constantly, until marshmallows are melted. Remove from heat. Stir in peppermint extract and a few drops of red food coloring, if desired. Pour into a metal bowl. Chill until mixture begins to thicken, stirring occasionally.

When marshmallow mixture is ready, beat the egg whites with an electric mixer until soft peaks form. Add 3 tablespoons sugar very gradually, beating constantly, until stiff peaks form. Fold egg whites into marshmallow mixture. Fold in the thawed whipped topping. Chill, if necessary, until filling mounds when spooned (about 30 minutes). Spoon filling into prepared crumb crust, cover, and chill for at least 4 hours (or overnight, if desired), until set. Makes 8 servings.

NUTRITION (PER SERVING): 163 CALORIES

TOTAL FAT	4 g	(19% OF CALORIES)
PROTEIN	3 g	(7% OF CALORIES)
CARBOHYDRATES	30 g	(74% OF CALORIES)
CHOLESTEROL	9 mg	
SODIUM	65 mg	

Cream Puffs or Eclairs

Pictured on page 143.

½ cup flour
¼ cup cornstarch
1 cup water
5 tablespoons margarine
3 eggs
Creamy Vanilla Pudding (recipe follows)

Spray a large baking sheet with nonstick cooking spray; set aside.

Mix together flour and cornstarch. Place water and margarine in a medium saucepan. Bring to a full rolling boil over medium–high heat. Reduce heat to medium low and add the flour mixture to the boiling water all at once, stirring briskly with a wooden spoon until mixture forms a ball. Remove from heat and cool for 2 minutes. Add eggs and beat with wooden spoon for 3 to 5 minutes or until the mixture is smooth.

For cream puffs, drop heaping tablespoons of batter at least 2 inches apart on prepared baking sheet. For eclairs, shape dough into narrow "fingers" about 3½ inches long, spaced 2 inches apart on baking sheet. Bake at 400 degrees F. for 10 minutes. Without opening oven door, reduce heat to 350 degrees F. and continue baking for 25 minutes longer or until puffs are golden brown. Remove from pan and cool to room temperature on wire racks.

Using a serrated knife, carefully slice tops off puffs or eclairs. Scoop out any filaments of uncooked dough. Fill with Creamy Vanilla Pudding and replace tops. Chill until ready to serve. For eclairs, frost if desired with Chocolate Glaze (page 127). Makes 15.

NUTRITION (PER SERVING): 110 CALORIES

TOTAL FAT	6 g	(50% OF CALORIES)
PROTEIN	3 g	(10% OF CALORIES)
CARBOHYDRATES	11 g	(40% OF CALORIES)
CHOLESTEROL	43 mg	
SODIUM	14 mg	

Creamy Vanilla Pudding

2 cups 2% low-fat milk
¼ cup sugar
2 tablespoons cornstarch
¼ teaspoon salt
1 teaspoon vanilla

Heat milk in the top of a double boiler until very hot. Combine sugar, cornstarch, and salt in a small bowl and stir in ½ cup of the hot milk. Stir until sugar is dissolved. Add sugar mixture slowly to the hot milk in double boiler, stirring constantly. Cook and stir until mixture thickens and is smooth, about 3 minutes. Cover and cook 5 minutes longer. Remove from heat and stir in vanilla. Cover with plastic wrap and let stand until cool. Refrigerate for 3 hours before serving. Makes 4 servings of pudding, or fills one batch of cream puffs or eclairs, or makes one 9-inch pie.

Variations

Chocolate Pudding or Pie Filling: Increase sugar to ⅓ cup, and cornstarch to 3 tablespoons. Add 2 squares melted unsweetened chocolate to the hot cooked pudding.

Banana Cream Pie: Add sliced bananas to cooled pudding; pour into baked pie shell.

Coconut Cream Pie: Stir ¾ cup flaked coconut into cooled pudding. Sprinkle an additional ¼ cup of coconut in the bottom of a baked pie shell and top with filling.

NUTRITION (PER SERVING IF PREPARED
AS VANILLA PUDDING):   127 CALORIES

TOTAL FAT	2 g	(17% OF CALORIES)
PROTEIN	4 g	(13% OF CALORIES)
CARBOHYDRATES	22 g	(70% OF CALORIES)
CHOLESTEROL	9 mg	
SODIUM	208 mg	

Chocolate Meringue Puff

3 egg whites
1 teaspoon vanilla
¼ teaspoon cream of tartar
1½ cups sugar, divided
¼ cup cornstarch
¼ cup cocoa
2½ cups skim milk
1½ teaspoons vanilla

Cover a baking sheet with plain brown paper. Draw a 9-inch circle on the paper; set aside.

In a mixing bowl, combine egg whites, 1 teaspoon vanilla, and cream of tartar. Beat with an electric mixer on medium speed until soft peaks form. Gradually add 1 cup sugar, beating on high speed about 4 minutes or until mixture forms stiff, glossy peaks and sugar is dissolved. Pipe mixture through a pastry tube onto the circle on the paper, building up the sides to form a shell. Bake at 300 degrees F. for 45 minutes. Turn off heat and let meringue shell dry in oven with door closed for 1 hour. Remove from pan and complete cooling on a wire rack.

Meanwhile, in a heavy saucepan combine ½ cup sugar, cornstarch, and cocoa. Stir in milk. Cook and stir over medium heat until thickened and bubbly; continue cooking, stirring constantly, 2 minutes more. Remove from heat. Stir in 1½ teaspoons vanilla. Cover surface with plastic wrap. Cool slightly without stirring, about 20 minutes. Pour into cooled meringue shell. Cover and chill thoroughly. If desired, garnish with low-fat whipped topping and fresh mint leaves. Makes 8 servings.

NUTRITION (PER SERVING): 209 CALORIES

TOTAL FAT	1 g	(2% OF CALORIES)
PROTEIN	4 g	(9% OF CALORIES)
CARBOHYDRATES	47 g	(89% OF CALORIES)
CHOLESTEROL	2 mg	
SODIUM	87 mg	

Peach and Blueberry Crisp

2 tablespoons granulated sugar
1 tablespoon flour
½ teaspoon cinnamon
¼ teaspoon nutmeg
4 peaches, pitted and sliced
1½ cups fresh or frozen blueberries
½ cup quick-cooking rolled oats
⅓ cup firmly packed brown sugar
3 tablespoons flour
2 tablespoons light butter
2 tablespoons toasted pecan pieces

In a small bowl, combine granulated sugar, 1 tablespoon flour, cinnamon, and nutmeg. Place the sliced peaches and blueberries in a 9-inch pie plate. Sprinkle sugar mixture over fruit; toss gently to coat.

Stir together oats, brown sugar, and 3 tablespoons flour. Cut in butter with a fork or pastry blender until mixture is crumbly. Stir in toasted pecans. Sprinkle over fruit mixture.

Bake at 375 degrees F. for 35 minutes or until fruit is tender and center is bubbly. If necessary, cover with foil during the last 10 minutes of baking to prevent overbrowning. Serve warm. Makes 6 servings.

NUTRITION (PER SERVING): 191 CALORIES

TOTAL FAT	4 g	(20% OF CALORIES)
PROTEIN	2 g	(5% OF CALORIES)
CARBOHYDRATES	35 g	(74% OF CALORIES)
CHOLESTEROL	5 mg	
SODIUM	29 mg	

Chocolate and Fresh Fruit Trifle (page 151), Cream Puffs and Eclairs (page 141)

European Blueberry Cobbler

1½ cups fresh or frozen blueberries
1 teaspoon sugar
⅔ cup skim milk
⅓ cup flour
1 egg
2 tablespoons sugar
1 teaspoon finely shredded orange peel
2 teaspoons vanilla
¼ teaspoon cinnamon
1 teaspoon sugar

Spray a 1½-quart shallow baking dish with nonstick cooking spray; set aside.

Mix blueberries with 1 teaspoon sugar in a medium bowl. Let stand, uncovered, at room temperature for 30 minutes.

Combine milk, flour, egg, 2 tablespoons sugar, orange peel, vanilla, and cinnamon in the container of an electric blender or food processor. Mix until smooth.

Arrange the blueberries evenly in the bottom of the prepared baking dish. Pour batter over the top, then sprinkle with 1 teaspoon sugar. Bake at 350 degrees F. for 1 hour or until golden brown. Makes 4 servings.

NUTRITION (PER SERVING): 148 CALORIES

TOTAL FAT	2 g	(10% OF CALORIES)
PROTEIN	4 g	(12% OF CALORIES)
CARBOHYDRATES	29 g	(78% OF CALORIES)
CHOLESTEROL	54 mg	
SODIUM	40 mg	

Good-Morning Pie

½ cup butter or margarine
1 cup sugar
1 cup flour
2 teaspoons baking powder
½ teaspoon salt
¾ cup skim milk
1 quart canned fruit packed in juice (your choice)

Preheat oven to 350 degrees. Melt butter or margarine in a 13 x 9-inch baking pan. Sift together the sugar, flour, baking powder, and salt. Add milk and stir until well blended. Pour over melted butter in baking pan (do not stir into butter). Pour fruit and juice over flour mixture (again, do not stir). Bake for 1 hour. Serve warm. Makes 15 servings.

NUTRITION (PER SERVING): 179 CALORIES

TOTAL FAT	6 g	(32% OF CALORIES)
PROTEIN	2 g	(4% OF CALORIES)
CARBOHYDRATES	29 g	(64% OF CALORIES)
CHOLESTEROL	17 mg	
SODIUM	198 mg	

Peach Kuchen

Batter

1 ¼ cups flour
1 teaspoon baking powder
½ teaspoon baking soda
¼ teaspoon salt
¼ teaspoon ginger
¼ teaspoon cinnamon
6 ½ tablespoons granulated sugar
2 tablespoons butter or margarine
1 egg
2 teaspoons vanilla
⅛ teaspoon almond extract
½ cup nonfat plain yogurt

Topping

⅓ cup flour
⅓ cup firmly packed brown sugar
2 tablespoons granulated sugar
¼ teaspoon cinnamon
1 ½ tablespoons butter or margarine,
    chilled and cut into small pieces
6 large peaches, peeled and coarsely sliced

Preheat oven to 375 degrees F. Spray an 11 x 7-inch baking dish with nonstick cooking spray; set aside.

Make batter: Sift together flour, baking powder, baking soda, salt, ginger, and cinnamon. In a medium mixer bowl, cream together sugar and butter or margarine. Add egg, vanilla, and almond extract; continue beating until light. Blend in the yogurt until thoroughly mixed. Add the flour mixture and stir just until moistened; do not overmix. Spread batter evenly in prepared baking dish.

Make topping: Combine flour, brown sugar, granulated sugar, and cinnamon. Cut in butter or margarine until mixture is crumbly. Sprinkle about ⅓ of the crumb mixture over the batter. Arrange peach slices evenly over the top, patting them down gently. Sprinkle with remaining crumb mixture. Bake for 30 minutes or until top is golden and bubbly and a toothpick inserted in center comes out clean. Place dish on a wire rack and let stand at least 10 minutes before cutting. Makes 8 servings.

NUTRITION (PER SERVING): 274 CALORIES

TOTAL FAT	6 g	(20% OF CALORIES)
PROTEIN	5 g	(7% OF CALORIES)
CARBOHYDRATES	50 g	(73% OF CALORIES)
CHOLESTEROL	40 mg	
SODIUM	242 mg	

Apple Cranberry Crisp

5 cups peeled sliced apples
1 cup cranberries
2 tablespoons granulated sugar
½ cup quick-cooking rolled oats
⅓ cup firmly packed brown sugar
3 tablespoons flour
½ teaspoon cinnamon
2 tablespoons light butter
½ cup nonfat vanilla or lemon yogurt

Spray a 9-inch square baking dish with nonstick cooking spray. Toss together the apple slices, cranberries, and granulated sugar. Arrange in bottom of prepared baking dish.

In a small bowl, combine oats, brown sugar, flour, and cinnamon. Cut in butter until crumbly. Sprinkle oat mixture evenly over apple mixture.

Bake at 375 degrees F. for 30 to 35 minutes or until apples are tender. Serve warm with a dollop of vanilla or lemon yogurt. Makes 6 servings.

NUTRITION (PER SERVING): 198 CALORIES

TOTAL FAT	3 g	(13% OF CALORIES)
PROTEIN	3 g	(6% OF CALORIES)
CARBOHYDRATES	40 g	(81% OF CALORIES)
CHOLESTEROL	5 mg	
SODIUM	41 mg	

Baked Apple Dessert

6 medium apples, peeled and sliced
1 tablespoon granulated sugar
½ teaspoon cinnamon
½ cup firmly packed brown sugar
⅓ cup flour
⅛ teaspoon nutmeg
2 tablespoons light butter, melted

Spray a 2-quart baking dish with nonstick cooking spray. In a large bowl, toss apples with granulated sugar and cinnamon. Place in prepared baking dish. Bake, covered, at 350 degrees F. for 30 minutes.

In a small bowl, combine brown sugar, flour, and nutmeg. Add melted butter, stirring with a fork until mixture is crumbly. Uncover baking dish and sprinkle brown sugar mixture over apples. Bake 15 to 20 minutes more or until apples are tender. Serve warm. Makes 6 servings.

NUTRITION (PER SERVING): 246 CALORIES

TOTAL FAT	3 g	(10% OF CALORIES)
PROTEIN	1 g	(2% OF CALORIES)
CARBOHYDRATES	54 g	(88% OF CALORIES)
CHOLESTEROL	5 mg	
SODIUM	28 mg	

Tapioca Pudding

5 1/2 cups skim milk
2/3 cup sugar
1/3 cup quick-cooking tapioca
3 egg whites
1 whole egg
1 1/2 teaspoons vanilla

Combine milk, sugar, tapioca, egg whites, and egg in a large saucepan. Let stand at room temperature for 5 minutes, then place over medium heat and cook, stirring constantly, until mixture comes to a full boil. Stir in vanilla. Remove from heat and let stand for 20 minutes. Serve warm or chilled. Makes 6 servings.

NUTRITION (PER SERVING): 217 CALORIES

TOTAL FAT	1 g	(5% OF CALORIES)
PROTEIN	10 g	(19% OF CALORIES)
CARBOHYDRATES	41 g	(76% OF CALORIES)
CHOLESTEROL	39 mg	
SODIUM	153 mg	

Rice Pudding

2 cups 1% low-fat milk
1 small can (5 1/3 ounces) evaporated skim milk
1/2 cup raisins
Boiling water
1/2 cup sugar
1 tablespoon cornstarch
1/4 teaspoon salt
2 cups cooked rice
3 egg whites
2 tablespoons sugar
1/8 teaspoon nutmeg
1/8 teaspoon cinnamon
1 teaspoon vanilla

In a small saucepan, scald the milks together. Measure raisins into a strainer and set over boiling water just long enough to plump them. Combine 1/2 cup sugar, cornstarch, and salt in the top of a double boiler; blend well. Stir in hot milk, stirring constantly over medium heat until thick and smooth. Add rice; reheat to a full boil, stirring constantly, in double boiler. Remove from heat. Beat egg whites lightly with 2 tablespoons sugar. Pour a little of the hot mixture into egg–white mixture, stirring rapidly. Return egg mixture to hot milk and rice; stir over medium heat 1 to 2 minutes or until thickened. Remove from heat. Stir in plumped raisins, nutmeg, cinnamon, and vanilla. Chill. Makes 8 servings.

NUTRITION (PER SERVING): 220 CALORIES

TOTAL FAT	1 g	(4% OF CALORIES)
PROTEIN	7 g	(13% OF CALORIES)
CARBOHYDRATES	46 g	(83% OF CALORIES)
CHOLESTEROL	4 mg	
SODIUM	163 mg	

Apple Bread Pudding

3 slices whole-grain bread, cut into 1-inch cubes
1 apple, peeled, cored, and chopped
2 tablespoons raisins or chopped prunes
1 can (12 ounces) evaporated skim milk
5 egg whites
2 whole eggs
2 tablespoons sugar
½ teaspoon cinnamon
⅛ teaspoon nutmeg
Nutmeg Sauce (recipe follows)

Spray a 9-inch square baking dish with nonstick cooking spray. Arrange bread cubes, chopped apple, and raisins or prunes in bottom of dish.

In a medium mixing bowl, combine milk, egg whites, whole eggs, sugar, cinnamon, and nutmeg. Beat with an electric mixer on medium speed until well mixed. Pour over bread and fruits in baking dish; let stand for 10 minutes. Cover with foil and bake at 325 degrees F. for 20 minutes. Remove foil and bake for 20 to 25 minutes more, or until a knife inserted in center of pudding comes out clean. Place dish on wire rack to cool slightly. Serve pudding warm with Nutmeg Sauce (recipe follows). Makes 6 servings.

NUTRITION (PER SERVING): 156 CALORIES

TOTAL FAT	2 g	(13% OF CALORIES)
PROTEIN	10 g	(27% OF CALORIES)
CARBOHYDRATES	24 g	(61% OF CALORIES)
CHOLESTEROL	73 mg	
SODIUM	182 mg	

Nutmeg Sauce

⅔ cup sugar
1½ tablespoons cornstarch
⅛ teaspoon salt
1 cup boiling water
4 tablespoons butter-flavored granules
½ teaspoon nutmeg

In a medium saucepan, combine sugar, cornstarch, and salt. Gradually stir in boiling water. Add butter-flavored granules. Cook and stir over medium heat until mixture is thick and bubbly; continue cooking, stirring constantly, 2 minutes more. Remove from heat. Stir in nutmeg. Serve warm. Makes about 8 servings, 2 tablespoons each.

NUTRITION (PER SERVING): 73 CALORIES

TOTAL FAT	LESS THAN 1 g	(1% OF CALORIES)
PROTEIN	0 g	(0% OF CALORIES)
CARBOHYDRATES	18 g	(99% OF CALORIES)
CHOLESTEROL	0 mg	
SODIUM	38 mg	

Slow-Cooked Carrot Pudding

1 cup finely grated raw potatoes
1 cup grated raw carrots
1 cup flour
¼ cup olive oil
1 teaspoon cinnamon
1 teaspoon allspice
1 teaspoon nutmeg
1 cup sugar
1 teaspoon salt
1 teaspoon baking soda
1 cup raisins (½ cup dark and
*   ½ cup golden, if desired)*
½ cup walnut pieces

Spray the pot of a slow cooker with nonstick cooking spray. Mix all ingredients together in the order given and pour into prepared slow-cooker pot. Cook on medium setting (or low if cooker has no medium setting) for about 3 hours or until set. Makes 10 servings.

NUTRITION (PER SERVING):   290 CALORIES

TOTAL FAT	9 g	(29% OF CALORIES)
PROTEIN	3 g	(4% OF CALORIES)
CARBOHYDRATES	48 g	(66% OF CALORIES)
CHOLESTEROL	0 mg	
SODIUM	326 mg	

Almond Rice Pudding

2 cups skim milk
½ cup uncooked rice
1 envelope unflavored gelatin
¼ cup cold water
¼ cup chopped blanched almonds
1 teaspoon vanilla
½ teaspoon almond extract
5 tablespoons sugar
¼ teaspoon salt
1½ cups evaporated skim milk

In a medium saucepan, bring skim milk to a boil over medium-high heat. Add rice; reduce heat and simmer, covered, until rice is tender, about 20 to 25 minutes. Dissolve gelatin in water. Stir into rice the gelatin, almonds, vanilla, almond extract, sugar, and salt. Cool slightly. Stir in evaporated skim milk. Refrigerate until well chilled. Makes 8 servings.

NUTRITION (PER SERVING):   164 CALORIES

TOTAL FAT	3 g	(15% OF CALORIES)
PROTEIN	8 g	(20% OF CALORIES)
CARBOHYDRATES	27 g	(65% OF CALORIES)
CHOLESTEROL	3 mg	
SODIUM	61 mg	

Baked Custard

8 egg whites, lightly beaten
2¾ cups 1% low-fat milk
½ cup evaporated skim milk
¼ cup sugar
¼ teaspoon salt
¾ teaspoon vanilla
¼ teaspoon yellow food coloring (optional)
⅛ teaspoon nutmeg (optional)

Beat egg whites; add milks, sugar, salt, vanilla, and food coloring, if desired. Strain into individual custard cups set into a pan of hot water. Sprinkle nutmeg on custard, if desired. Bake at 350 degrees F. for 40 to 50 minutes. Custard is cooked when knife inserted near center comes out clean. Remove from water to cool. Chill and serve in cups. Makes 8 servings.

Note: Custard may be baked in a 1½- or 2-quart casserole dish instead of in individual cups. Bake for about 50 minutes.

NUTRITION (PER SERVING): 88 CALORIES

TOTAL FAT	1 g	(9% OF CALORIES)
PROTEIN	7 g	(34% OF CALORIES)
CARBOHYDRATES	13 g	(57% OF CALORIES)
CHOLESTEROL	4 mg	
SODIUM	189 mg	

Chocolate and Fresh Fruit Trifle

Pictured on page 143.

1 angel food cake
1 package (3½ ounces) instant
    chocolate fudge pudding mix
2 cups skim milk
1 teaspoon vanilla
2 cups assorted sliced fresh fruit: bananas,
    nectarines, peaches, pineapple, strawberries,
    raspberries, or other choices
1 cup light whipped topping
1 tablespoon grated chocolate
1 tablespoon sliced almonds

Cut cake in ¾-inch cubes. Place half the cubes in the bottom of a large clear glass bowl. Prepare pudding as directed on package, using 2 cups of skim milk. Stir in vanilla. Spoon half of pudding on top of cake cubes; arrange half of fruit on top of pudding. Repeat layers, ending with fruit. Top with whipped topping. Cover and refrigerate until thoroughly chilled, at least 1 hour. Just before serving, top with grated chocolate and slivered almonds. Makes 16 servings.

NUTRITION (PER SERVING): 58 CALORIES

TOTAL FAT	1 g	(18% OF CALORIES)
PROTEIN	2 g	(10% OF CALORIES)
CARBOHYDRATES	10 g	(71% OF CALORIES)
CHOLESTEROL	1 mg	
SODIUM	43 mg	

Strawberry-Banana Sorbet

1 medium ripe banana
3 cups frozen unsweetened strawberries
½ cup frozen concentrated cranberry-juice cocktail
1 tablespoon light corn syrup

Wrap peeled banana in plastic and freeze until solid (at least 2 hours). In a food processor or blender, puree the strawberries until very smooth. Add the juice concentrate and continue blending until smooth, about 1 minute. Slice the frozen banana and add slices a few at a time, continuing to blend until completely smooth. Blend in corn syrup. May be served immediately, or place in a chilled bowl, covered, and frozen for 30 minutes. Sorbet will keep in freezer for up to 1 week; let soften slightly before serving. Makes 6 servings.

NUTRITION (PER SERVING): 71 CALORIES

TOTAL FAT	LESS THAN 1 g	(2% OF CALORIES)
PROTEIN	1 g	(5% OF CALORIES)
CARBOHYDRATES	17 g	(95% OF CALORIES)
CHOLESTEROL	0 mg	
SODIUM	5 mg	

Fresh Grapefruit Sorbet

½ cup cold water
1 teaspoon unflavored gelatin powder
⅔ cup diced pink grapefruit sections
1 cup pink grapefruit juice
⅓ cup sugar
1 tablespoon lemon juice

In a large saucepan, combine cold water and gelatin. Cook and stir over low heat until gelatin is dissolved. Remove from heat and stir in diced grapefruit, grapefruit juice, sugar, and lemon juice. Pour into ice-cube trays or an 8-inch square baking pan, and freeze until almost firm.

Break frozen mixture into chunks and place in blender or food processor. Blend several seconds, until fluffy but not thawed. Return to freezer trays and freeze until firm. Makes 6 servings.

NUTRITION (PER SERVING): 61 CALORIES

TOTAL FAT	LESS THAN 1 g	(1% OF CALORIES)
PROTEIN	1 g	(7% OF CALORIES)
CARBOHYDRATES	14 g	(92% OF CALORIES)
CHOLESTEROL	0 mg	
SODIUM	1 mg	

Melon Sorbet

1 cup orange juice
¼ cup sugar
2 cups chopped cantaloupe,
    honeydew, or watermelon
½ cup light cream
3 tablespoons lemon juice
Food coloring, if desired
2 egg whites
¼ cup sugar

Bring orange juice and ¼ cup sugar to boil in a small saucepan over medium-high heat, stirring occasionally. Reduce heat to low; simmer for 5 minutes. Cool. Blend melon and light cream in a blender or food processor until smooth, about 1 minute. Stir in the lemon juice and cooled orange juice mixture. If using honeydew, you may wish to add a few drops of green food coloring; for watermelon, use red food coloring, if desired. Pour mixture into a 9-inch square baking pan; cover and freeze until firm, about 4 hours. Chill a mixer bowl during this time for use later.

Using an electric mixer, beat egg whites until soft peaks form. Gradually add ¼ cup sugar, beating until stiff peaks form.

Place frozen mixture in chilled mixer bowl. Break into chunks and beat with electric mixer until fluffy but not melted. Fold in beaten egg whites. Return to baking pan. Cover and freeze for several hours or until firm. Remove from freezer about 5 minutes before serving to soften slightly. Makes 6 servings.

NUTRITION (PER SERVING):   174 CALORIES

TOTAL FAT	6 g	(33% OF CALORIES)
PROTEIN	2 g	(6% OF CALORIES)
CARBOHYDRATES	27 g	(61% OF CALORIES)
CHOLESTEROL	22 mg	
SODIUM	31 mg	

Creamy Pineapple Sherbet

¼ cup sugar
1 envelope unflavored gelatin
½ cup water
1 canned (15 ounces) crushed pineapple
    in juice, undrained
⅔ cup sugar
2 tablespoons honey
1 teaspoon vanilla
2 cups nonfat buttermilk

In a small saucepan, stir together ¼ cup sugar and gelatin; add water. Cook and stir over low heat until sugar and gelatin are dissolved. Remove from heat and cool the mixture slightly.

In a blender or food processor, combine pineapple with juice, ⅔ cup sugar, honey, vanilla, and gelatin mixture. Cover and blend until smooth. Stir in buttermilk.

Freeze the mixture in a 4-quart ice-cream freezer according to the manufacturer's directions. Makes 12 servings.

NUTRITION (PER SERVING):   109 CALORIES

TOTAL FAT	0 g	(3% OF CALORIES)
PROTEIN	2 g	(7% OF CALORIES)
CARBOHYDRATES	24 g	(89% OF CALORIES)
CHOLESTEROL	1 mg	
SODIUM	44 mg	

Frozen Fruit Dessert

12 foil cupcake papers
2 medium ripe bananas
1 cup fresh or frozen strawberries
1 small can (8 ounces) crushed pineapple, drained
2 tablespoons honey
1 dash nutmeg
1 cup light whipped topping
¼ cup chopped almonds
1 tablespoon cornstarch
1 tablespoon sugar
1 cup cherry juice
Fresh fruit for garnish (optional)

Place foil cupcake papers in 12 muffin cups. In a blender or food processor, combine bananas, strawberries, pineapple, honey, and nutmeg. Blend until smooth. Fold in whipped topping and almonds; pour into prepared muffin cups. Cover and freeze about 4 hours or until firm.

In a small saucepan, combine cornstarch and sugar. Stir in cherry juice. Cook over medium heat, stirring constantly, until sauce thickens and bubbles. Cool.

To serve, spoon cherry sauce onto individual dessert plates. Remove desserts from foil liners and invert on top of sauce. Garnish with fresh fruit, if desired. Makes 12 servings.

NUTRITION (PER SERVING): 89 CALORIES

TOTAL FAT	2 g	(24% OF CALORIES)
PROTEIN	1 g	(5% OF CALORIES)
CARBOHYDRATES	16 g	(71% OF CALORIES)
CHOLESTEROL	0 mg	
SODIUM	2 mg	

Fresh Peach Dessert

¾ cup crushed vanilla wafer cookies
* (about 12 wafers)*
1 tablespoon butter or margarine, melted
¼ teaspoon cinnamon
¼ cup sugar
3 tablespoons cornstarch
12 ounces peach nectar
1 tablespoon lemon juice
¼ teaspoon almond extract
⅛ teaspoon nutmeg
4 cups peeled, sliced fresh peaches
1 cup low-fat vanilla yogurt

Preheat oven to 375 degrees F. Mix together crushed cookies, melted butter or margarine, and cinnamon, stirring well to coat crumbs. Spread on a baking sheet. Bake until lightly toasted, about 7 minutes. Set aside.

In a large saucepan, thoroughly combine sugar and cornstarch. Stir in peach nectar, lemon juice, almond extract, and nutmeg; bring to a boil over medium-high heat. Reduce heat to low and simmer, stirring constantly, until mixture is clear and thickened. Remove from heat and let cool. Gently stir in peaches.

Arrange 8 individual dessert dishes on a tray. Place half the cookie crumbs in the dishes and top with half the peach mixture. Repeat layers. Cover and chill for at least 2 hours. Just before serving, top each dessert with 2 tablespoons vanilla yogurt. Makes 8 servings.

NUTRITION (PER SERVING): 148 CALORIES

TOTAL FAT	3 g	(17% OF CALORIES)
PROTEIN	2 g	(6% OF CALORIES)
CARBOHYDRATES	29 g	(77% OF CALORIES)
CHOLESTEROL	7 mg	
SODIUM	47 mg	

Baked Pears with Caramel Sauce

6 ripe pears
3 tablespoons finely chopped pecans
½ teaspoon grated lemon peel
¼ cup firmly packed brown sugar
3 tablespoons dark corn syrup
¼ cup water
1 teaspoon butter or margarine

Preheat oven to 350 degrees F. Core pears from the bottom, leaving stem ends intact. Mix pecans and lemon peel; pack mixture evenly into cavities of pears. Arrange pears, stem ends up, in an ungreased 3-quart baking dish. Add water to a depth of 1 inch. Cover and bake for 50 minutes or until pears are tender.

In a small saucepan, combine brown sugar, corn syrup, ¼ cup water, and butter or margarine. Bring to a boil, stirring constantly until sugar is dissolved. Boil gently, stirring frequently, for an additional 5 minutes. Place warm pears in individual dessert dishes and pour sauce over the tops. Makes 6 servings.

NUTRITION (PER SERVING): 203 CALORIES

TOTAL FAT	4 g	(17% OF CALORIES)
PROTEIN	1 g	(2% OF CALORIES)
CARBOHYDRATES	41 g	(82% OF CALORIES)
CHOLESTEROL	2 mg	
SODIUM	16 mg	

Fruit Ambrosia

1 package instant sugar-free vanilla pudding mix
2 cups skim milk
1 tablespoon lemon juice
1 teaspoon grated lemon peel
¼ teaspoon almond or coconut extract
1 small can (8 ounces) pineapple tidbits, drained
1 cup assorted sliced fresh fruit (bananas, strawberries, peaches, or other choice)
¼ cup miniature marshmallows

In a medium bowl, make pudding with skim milk according to package directions. Stir in lemon juice, lemon peel, and extract.

Divide pudding evenly among 4 individual dessert bowls, reserving ¼ cup for topping. Combine fruits and marshmallows; spoon into bowls on top of pudding. Drizzle with reserved pudding. Makes 4 servings.

NUTRITION (PER SERVING): 169 CALORIES

TOTAL FAT	1 g	(5% OF CALORIES)
PROTEIN	5 g	(12% OF CALORIES)
CARBOHYDRATES	35 g	(83% OF CALORIES)
CHOLESTEROL	2 mg	
SODIUM	396 mg	

Sugar-Free Raspberry Topping

1 pint fresh raspberries, divided
1/4 cup unsweetened apple juice
2 tablespoons frozen unsweetened
    apple juice concentrate
2 teaspoons cornstarch
1/4 teaspoon vanilla

Place 1 cup of the berries with the apple juice in a blender. Puree until smooth. In a small saucepan, stir together apple juice concentrate and cornstarch until smooth. Add pureed berry mixture. Cook over low heat, stirring constantly, until mixture thickens. Cool. Stir in remaining raspberries and vanilla. Serve over nonfat frozen yogurt or pancakes. Makes 12 servings, about 2 tablespoons each.

NUTRITION (PER SERVING): 16 CALORIES

TOTAL FAT	0 g	(0% OF CALORIES)
PROTEIN	0 g	(0% OF CALORIES)
CARBOHYDRATES	4 g	(100% OF CALORIES)
CHOLESTEROL	0 mg	
SODIUM	1 mg	

Apricot Nectar Shake

1 cup chilled apricot nectar
2 teaspoons lemon juice
1 pinch salt
1 cup vanilla ice milk

Blend apricot nectar with lemon juice and salt in blender. Add ice milk and blend to desired consistency. Serve immediately. Makes 4 servings.

NUTRITION (PER SERVING): 95 CALORIES

TOTAL FAT	1 g	(11% OF CALORIES)
PROTEIN	2 g	(9% OF CALORIES)
CARBOHYDRATES	19 g	(79% OF CALORIES)
CHOLESTEROL	3 mg	
SODIUM	140 mg	

Butterscotch Sauce

1 1/2 cups brown sugar
3/4 cup light corn syrup
1/8 teaspoon salt
1 cup evaporated skim milk

Combine brown sugar, corn syrup, and salt in a medium saucepan; cook over medium heat, stirring constantly, until sugar dissolves. Gradually add evaporated milk. Continue cooking and stirring until thickened. Serve hot over nonfat frozen yogurt or steamed puddings. Makes 16 servings, about 2 tablespoons each.

NUTRITION (PER SERVING): 140 CALORIES

TOTAL FAT	0 g	(0% OF CALORIES)
PROTEIN	1 g	(3% OF CALORIES)
CARBOHYDRATES	34 g	(97% OF CALORIES)
CHOLESTEROL	0 mg	
SODIUM	1 mg	

INDEX